I0631520

Glass House Books

And Other Essays

For the last couple of decades, Michael Cohen has been publishing personal and topical essays in a variety of magazines from the *Harvard Review* to *Birding*. IP published a collection of them, *A Place to Read*, in 2014. Here is another collection, *And Other Essays*.

Before he retired from teaching, Cohen wrote an introductory poetry text, *The Poem in Question* (Harcourt Brace, 1983) and an award winning Shakespeare study, *Hamlet in My Mind's Eye* (Georgia, 1989).

Michael Cohen lives in Lincoln, Nebraska.

And Other Essays

Michael Cohen

Glass House Books
Brisbane

Glass House Books
an imprint of IP (Interactive Publications Pty Ltd)
Treetop Studio • 9 Kuhler Court
Carindale, Queensland, Australia 4152
sales@ipoz.biz
http://ipoz.biz

© 2020, IP and Michael Cohen
eBook versions © 2020

Printed in 12 pt Adobe Caslon Pro on 16 pt Avenir Book.

ISBN: 9781922332257 (PB); 9781922332264 (eBk)

a catalogue record of this book is available
from the National Library of Australia

Contents

Acknowledgements

Cover image: Dan Cohen. "Muir Woods"

Book design: David Reiter

A list of acknowledgements of the books I've cited or discussed follows these essays. The list also acknowledges the magazines that first published my essays. But here I happily acknowledge with love those who've given my writing the critical look it sorely needed: Katharine Weston Cohen, Matt Cohen, Nicole Gray, and Dan Cohen, all good writers themselves, who have worked hard to save me from the unintelligible, the badly argued, and the dumb.

Preface

This is an unapologetically bookish sort of book. Scores of books are mentioned here, and I discuss quite a few in detail. I don't have much patience with people who believe the only real knowledge comes from experience and not from books. Most of what I've learned in almost eight decades has been mediated by my reading if it hasn't come directly from the printed page. Reading is, in the final analysis, but another, more condensed and organized form of experience. Keats's reading took him to "realms of gold," and Borges said reading a book was "no less an experience than traveling or falling in love." Reading expands life experience, and life experience improves reading.

Most of the essays I write seem to follow the standard advice to write about what I know: the fun of flying small planes, the joys and jolts of family, writing itself, playing golf, eating good food, going often to the gym, traveling—but the greatest extender of what I know is reading. And sometimes reading takes me way beyond the sphere of my other experiences. In the essay below called "The God Damners," for example, I'm looking at the more outspoken atheists and their attack, not just on fundamentalism and radical extremist religion, but on theism itself. I was particularly trying to understand why the books of the so-called "New Atheists" so resonated with the American reading public in the first decade of the twenty-first century; these writers produced at least six best sellers between 2004 and 2007.

Also literally out of my comfort zone was the subject matter of "Agonists"; namely, writers who perform their own grief and suffering on the page. Nancy Mairs wrote of her readers, "I want them to wince." Had I not happened to read Joan Didion's *The Year of Magical Thinking*, I would probably never have read works by Mairs, Dubus, and others included in my essay.

Even my new experiences that do not begin with reading have a way of moving quickly toward the written word. I describe encounters with southern border crossers in "South Texas Diary, 2006." And my brother's suicide led me through grief and self-doubt and eventually to the slightly odd tone of "Advice on Writing Your Suicide Note." Surprise encounters with illegal immigrants are mulled over in the form of a diary; a tragic suicide gets transformed into an ironic writing prompt. For me reading is a form of doing, but the other side of that is the constant transformation of nonverbal experience into words, sentences, essays. Writing is also experience. I read to know and write to discover what I think about it all.

Don't Read the Whole Thing

John Rawls, introducing his influential *A Theory of Justice*, does a remarkable thing for an author. "This is a long book," he writes, and then proceeds to explain how you can get the theory he presents along with explanations of terms and pertinent examples by reading sections of the book that amount to only about a third of his 600 pages! It would be churlish not to take this advice, I thought, choosing the 200-page option. Plenty of other books, in my opinion—famous ones, classics, and supposed must-reads—should be preceded by Rawls-like advice about how to read them without reading all of them.

According to Sir Francis Bacon, "Some books are to be tasted, others to be swallowed, and some few to be chewed and digested." Yes, even the classics may need some selective tasting. By all means read every word of *The Odyssey*, the master narrative of Western literature, because it will entertain, and, if you are a storyteller, train you as well. But *The Iliad* is another matter. When Homer describes encounters between Paris and Hector or Hector and Andromache, still more when he turns his merciless attention to Trojans and Greeks killing each other, he will keep anyone's interest. But if you read every item in his catalogues of which country sent how many ships to Troy, only if you have a map of ancient city-states before you and a passion for ancient geography will you stay awake. By all means, skim Homer's lists as you would the begats in Genesis. Just keep in mind that Homer's catalogues really did interest his first readers and still command the attention of students of the ancient world.

The Aeneid requires cutting on a different plan. Here it's pretty much a matter of checking out after the councils of the gods in Book 1, the escape from Troy in 2, Aeneas's travels in 3, the romance of Dido and Aeneas in 4, and the trip to the Underworld in 6. In 6 we get a prophecy of what happens until the founding of Rome, but we don't have to actually live through the enactment of the prophecy.

Authors may not be as helpful as John Rawls, but they do sometimes signal where your attention can wander. When a shepherd in *Don Quixote* begins to tell a story peopled by no one we've yet met but rather folks with conventional Romantic names, it's safe to skip the rest of that chapter and possibly the next; the chapter titles will tell us when the main narrative resumes.

The point is that life is short and some books—even some very good books—are too long. A lot of selective reading is just taste, of course. At the halfway point in *The Rise and Fall of the Third Reich* I realized that Hitler's monomaniacal hobbling of his generals' freedom to act and other aspects of the war's progress were going to be far less interesting to me than the story of Hitler's complicated and politically astute climb to power had been, and I just stopped reading. It's your reading life, after all, and no one else's; find the good parts and leave the rest unread.

The Cross and the Windmills

Drivers on Interstate 40, coming over a low hill on the Texas plains east of Amarillo, see on the horizon a white cross. The town nearby is Groom, with about six hundred residents, located on a bypass from the interstate, a little piece of the old Route 66. The cross, when it suddenly appeared on the horizon and grew gradually bigger as I approached, was until recently an imposing and isolated sight, dominating an otherwise empty landscape. Since the cross is visible for nearly ten miles, there is a lot of time to wonder at its presence, to speculate on exactly how big it is and who erected it. I discovered the answers to these questions by pulling into the small park next to the cross and reading the information posted there.

The cross is almost sixty meters high—190 feet to be exact, or as tall as a 15-story building. Its arms stretch 110 feet. For comparison, the statue of *Christ the Redeemer* that looks out over Rio de Janeiro from the top of Corcovado Mountain is only 30 meters tall, though it has the advantage of Corcovado's 700-meter height to give it prominence. The stylized corrugations representing folds in the robe in Paul Landowski's Art Deco design for *Cristo Redentor* may possibly have suggested the fluting or channeling in the skin of the Groom cross. Two Texas millionaires are responsible for the cross. Chris Britten, who owned the large, now defunct gas station, curio shop, and restaurant nearby, donated the land, and Steve Thomas had the cross built in sections in Pampa, Texas, before it was transported and assembled at this site in 1995. Bronze statues representing the stations of the cross and other sacred subjects ring the white metal cross. These include a *pietá* copied from Michelangelo, a St. Michael and Lucifer that could be mistaken for St. George and the Dragon, a fountain, an empty tomb, an anti-abortion monument, and the ten commandments. But the main player is the cross, dwarfing all the bronze below. Yet it is almost an anticlimax to arrive at the cross, since we can only imagine its size, with nothing to provide scale, during our approach to it, and it could, for all we could guess from ten or five miles away, be four hundred feet tall.

Not long ago as I drove on I-40, approaching the cross at Groom, I saw on the horizon white shapes of a very different sort, dozens of them, and all larger than the Groom cross. They were the huge three-bladed windmills or wind turbines that we have become accustomed to seeing over the last few years on the windy plains of America. Cross and turbines have in common a certain mysteriousness of scale: I find it difficult, even when I am within a few hundred yards, to guess how large they are. But I have often seen on the road trucks transporting the blades of turbines, and with cars for comparison I have no trouble comprehending that each blade is over a hundred feet long.

In fact the blades are 130 feet long, and the tower that supports them is over two hundred fifty feet high, so the structure, when a blade is pointing straight up, is easily four hundred feet tall, or more than twice the height of the Groom cross, and there are dozens of them in view as one approaches and drives by the cross. The wind turbines (so-called even though they are not actually turbines but simple generators powered by the geared-up turning of a wind fan) are often arranged along the fronts of mesas so that they look like modern equivalents of the windmills of La Mancha, and I can imagine that some wizard—Frestón, for instance—had replaced the old landmarks with these three-armed white giants. Wind farms, they call these collections, and some in America have almost five thousand of the turbines.

I have to think that at least part of the intent and effort of the two millionaires who put up the cross has been frustrated. The intent, I imagine, was at least partly to create a particular moment of contemplation of Christianity's central symbol and of what it means to those speeding toward it over the plains of the Texas Panhandle at seventy-five miles an hour.

Whether our thoughts were contemplative and religious, or whether, like me, you were merely marveling at the scale of the cross, it captured your thoughts for the time it took to reach it. It gestured upward from a terrain of flatness and clear views to a far horizon. Like Wallace Stevens's jar in Tennessee, the cross organized a natural landscape with the insertion of a man-made object and perhaps pointed thoughts toward a third realm beyond the physical.

But no more. What has happened here is partly dilution and partly distraction. Attention that once had been trained solely on the cross is now divided among a number of monumental shapes on the plain. An added distraction is the movement of the new shapes. An aesthetic question arises: is the cross more beautiful than the windmills, or vice versa? And beyond aesthetics is the question of meaning and meaningful activity: the cross does symbolic work while the wind turbines do real work. The many questions the turbines raise do not touch the metaphysical. Who put them up? Where does the electricity they generate get distributed, and how much juice is there? Does the wind always blow here? How long does it take for the electricity generated to pay off the cost of these huge machines? Wind turbines call us to the things of this world.

Talking to Myself

"You're gonna make me give myself a good talking-to."
– Bob Dylan, "You're Gonna Make Me Lonesome When You Go"

Coasting down Ironwood Hill Drive the other day, I saw in the sky ahead a dogfight between two birds. I managed to see the flash of rust that told me the chased flyer was a red-tailed hawk. The chaser was a much smaller bird, but I couldn't tell what it was. As I drove on, there went quickly through my head what seemed to be a dialogue, though only one voice was really articulated:

Curious: "Aren't you going to stop?"
Lazy: "-------?"
Curious: "All right, how many things are you going to happen on today as possibly interesting as this one?"
Lazy: "------!"

I pulled over, hit the hazard light button, grabbed the binoculars I keep handy, and jumped out. Nothing visible in the clear blue Arizona sky.

Curious: "Next time, react a little faster."
Lazy: "---- ---."

I've filled in Lazy's part of the dialogue with punctuated blanks, because I'm not really sure what that second interior voice said to the first one. In fact, I'm not really sure it was a conversation. Is it merely a convention or a metaphor when we call thinking like this a dialogue, a talk that I had with myself? Do you have to have a split personality to have a conversation with yourself? When you talk to yourself, does anyone answer?

*

I asked my wife Katharine whether she had conversations with herself and she said no, but working in the yard, she would occasionally ask her dad (gone these twenty years) about a tree or a shrub, "What should I do with this thing, Dad?"

"Does he answer?" I asked.

"No, but it's a way of trying to recall advice he might have given, a way to jog my own memory."

I hoped for some enlightenment for my question when I saw the title of a book that came out in 2016: *The Voices Within: The History and Science of How We Talk to Ourselves.* Charles Fernyhough, a psychologist at England's Durham University, is the author. Fernyhough has many questions about what we hear inside our heads, but not many answers. He presents a flawed and inadequate model that depends on research in the 1920s by Jean Piaget, modified by Lev Vygotsky and based on the observation of children: they communicate with others, and then they often use "private speech" when they are at play, asking themselves aloud what they plan to build or draw, answering their own questions, and elaborating. This thinking out loud is internalized as "inner speech," which becomes the origin of the dialogues we sometimes perform in our imaginations as well as the hallucinated voices that people with schizophrenia and other mental illnesses may hear. Fernyhough is candid in admitting that most researchers disagree with his model and think the voices in such people come from early trauma and repressed memory. But he persists. The famous physicist Richard Feynman, he tells us, reports real dialogue with himself in problem-solving:

"The integral will be larger than the sum of the terms, so that would make the pressure higher, you see?"

"No, you're crazy."

"No, I'm not! No, I'm not!"

No, he wasn't, said a voice in my head. No, he wasn't.

*

When you talk to yourself, does anyone answer? We all know of pathological instances. David Berkowitz, the infamous "Son of Sam" killer who murdered six people in New York City in 1976, claimed to have been ordered to kill people by the voice of his neighbor's dog and by his own gun; he had conversations with both. Most of us, I suspect, have had the experience of encountering on the street a person who may have a mental illness and who seems to be conversing with himself or herself. A psychiatrist friend of mine has told me that the continuous talking of many such people has the intention of trying to drown out or quiet the voices they are hearing.

Not everyone who hears voices is crazy. The Feynman example above seems to indicate that some people without mental illness can have a real dialogue and an answering voice. Another friend, a psychologist who studies auditory hallucinations, has told me that up to twenty-five percent of the population may hear voices in some form, from the simple case of thinking you've heard your name called while you're walking on a noisy city street to cases of people hearing the voice of a dead loved one speaking whole sentences.

In dreams, I've spoken with my own loved ones who have recently died and have been reassured and consoled by such conversations—but of course dreams are very different from our waking lives. A waking conversation with oneself means we supply both sides and remain conscious that we are doing it. And monologues are also different. I say aloud, over my putt, "Keep your head still, damn it!" Or addressing a drive, "Finish your backswing." When I soloed in a small plane I did not actually *see* my instructor in the seat next to me, but in my mind I clearly heard *his* voice: "Keep the nose down…watch the airspeed…square the turn to final…watch the airspeed."

*

Literary examples of internal dialogue or argument between parts of the psyche ("You're crazy! No, I'm not!") may not be as ancient as the Greek word used to name such dialogues: *Psychomachia* or battle of the spirit/soul; they seem instead to begin in the Christian era. A fifth-century poet, Prudentius, gave the title *Psychomachia* to his poem about the Christian virtues fighting and defeating the vices of Pride, Anger, Lust, and the threatening spirit of Paganism. In later centuries, Christian apologists use the form of the battle between vice and virtue in the soul of a struggling sinner hoping for salvation. Such a struggle makes up the conflict in the fifteenth-century morality play *Everyman* and the seventeenth-century allegorical novel *Pilgrim's Progress*, where the hero is named "Christian."

Shakespeare occasionally splits a character into two parts and dramatizes his or her internal debate in a soliloquy. Chilling examples occur in *Hamlet*. Thinking aloud—the very definition of a soliloquy—Hamlet poses the question: why not, given a hostile world and outrageous Fortune, take "quietus" with a "bare bodkin?" Another question answers the first: don't we fear what comes after and its unknowns? When Hamlet considers killing the praying Claudius, he first says he will do it, but an answer comes back, "And so he goes to heaven." That needs to be looked at a little closer, thinks Hamlet aloud. "And am I then revenged?" he asks, and answers his own question, "No!" He does not kill Claudius, even though the other question he asks—"how his audit stands who knows save heaven?"—means there is no guarantee that Claudius's appearance of repentance is real. And indeed, as soon as Hamlet moves on, Claudius admits his repentance is not genuine. Hamlet can be cold-blooded: Here half of him wants revenge by killing Claudius; the other half wants to *kill Claudius's soul*.

We might say Hamlet's interior dialogues aren't typical; he is, after all, the Young Man Who Can't Make Up His Mind. But to back away from this particular example to the idea of drama in general, it is a dialogic form that starts in ancient Greece with two voices in conflict. A playwright's job is to listen to the inner voices and get them onto the page while capturing their differences. His creative act reproduces a multiple personality disorder without the pathology.

Shakespeare's internal debaters—his speaker in "Sonnet 144" also talks about his "better angel" and his "worser spirit"—are not always so far from the good-versus-evil back and forth in dialogue, still with us in movies or TV commercials when a tiny angel perches on one shoulder of the conflicted young woman (should she have another wicked chocolate?) and an equally tiny devil speaks into her ear from the other shoulder. Sometimes the stakes are much higher: remember "the better angels of our nature" that Abraham Lincoln invokes in his first inaugural speech, suggesting that we have within us the impulses both for war and for peace.

*

Let me go back to the personal example with which I began, where two voices in my head debated about whether I should get off my duff and do some nature observing. I called the two voices "Curious" and "Lazy." But they might have been called, more pretentiously, "Industry" and "Sloth," whose struggle with each other would have been recognizable to John Bunyan or the author of *Everyman*. Internal dialogue, while it may be problem-solving as in the Feynman example, is more frequently an internal debate about what we ought to do versus what we'd rather do. And when it's not dialogue, it's just a one-way communication, the voice of conscience, the "still small voice" speaking to Elijah, the Dutch uncle in your mind roughly reminding you to call your mother or brother, or perhaps an admonitory voice you recognize as your mother telling you once again to be nice, do the right thing, lend a helping hand. In the *Apology*, Socrates claims to have a *daemonium*, a little spirit that warns him when he is about to do something he should not do. Why didn't he just admit that he could still hear his mom telling him to do the right thing?

*

William James devotes a hundred pages of *The Principles of Psychology* to "The Consciousness of Self, and his idea of the self includes those persons and things that I think of when I think of what is "mine." Thus, the self is extended to include others. But except for pathological cases he does not discuss talking to oneself or having conversations with oneself. For James, inner dialogue doesn't seem to be active in the healthy self. Recently, some psychologists have formulated "Dialogic Self Theory," a description of the self mainly associated with the Dutch psychologist Hubert Hermans, with the admitted influences of James and of Mikhail Bakhtin, who wrote about the "dialogic" imagination in Dostoevsky's novels and the novelist's aversion to a monolithic voice or authorial attitude as he attempted to reconcile opposing views in his characters. The self, according to Dialogic Self Theory, is "extended"—the word James used—and involves attitudes of family, friends, and colleagues which are internalized. The self may suppress these other views to present a monolithic posture to the world, but accepting other views in an internal dialogue allows for development and rejuvenation of the self. But the theory does not suggest the dialogues ever get to the level of an out-loud exchange ("You're crazy! No, I'm not!").

*

To leave theory behind, there are some studies that are encouraging to those of us who habitually talk to ourselves. Carol Marie Kronk in "Private Speech in Adolescents," published in the 1994 *Adolescence*; Daniel Swingley and Gary Lupyan in "Self-directed Speech Affects Visual Search Performance," in the 2011 *The Quarterly Journal of Experimental Psychology*; as well as psychologists and non-psychologists all over the blogosphere discuss talking to oneself as an aid to thinking, finding an object, making a decision, or improving one's self-esteem. This last only works if you say *good* things about yourself when you talk to yourself, as in Émile Coué's famous formula from the turn of the twentieth century: "Every day in every way, I am getting better and better."

Positive reinforcement isn't any great mystery. Darts players hit their targets more often if they say to themselves "I can do this" than when they say something negative, according to a study by four psychologists in the *International*

Research Journal of Applied and Basic Sciences published in 2012 titled "The Effect of Self-talk and Mental Imagery on Self-efficacy in Throwing Darts in Adolescents." Successful athletes give themselves pep talks or pieces of advice such as "keep your eye on the ball"—professional golfers call this a swing thought.

But why would saying a thought aloud take you closer to a problem's solution than merely thinking about it? One reason is that a clearer conception of the problem or the requirements of the answer may result from saying it aloud. Most problem-solving heuristics—the best one I know is still George Pólya's *How To Solve It*—insist that first you have to understand the problem and what you are being asked to find. As most teachers know, until you have tried to articulate something—speaking it aloud to yourself or to an audience—you may not actually know it.

Finally, in defense of talking to myself I offer this: speaking a thought aloud engages more of your brain, fires more neurons, than merely thinking it. We know from the studies mentioned above that speaking aloud the place you are putting something helps you remember its location later. The recollection *is* a kind of dialogue: "Now where did I put those keys?" and the reply is the memory of yourself, saying, "I am putting the keys on the kitchen counter."

My wife asks her father what to do with this plant and waits, not for a spoken answer exactly, but a surfacing memory: His voice saying "What I usually do is...." The voice, the memory, is evoked by initiating a conversation, even if an audible response is not expected. So, I suggest, if you are querying an absent father or just giving yourself a good talking-to, speak out. "Are you crazy? No, you're not!"

Why Didn't Our Big Brains Save Us?

Evidence accumulates confirming that we have passed the tipping point in our ineffective efforts to stop the deterioration of the planet's atmosphere caused by human beings. (See, for example, Jonathan Watts's article, "Domino-effect of climate events could move Earth into a "hothouse' state," in *The Guardian* for 7 August 2018; Watts summarizes a study published the previous day in *Proceedings of the National Academy of Sciences*. See also the daily news.) It seems as if our big brains ought to have saved us. The big forebrain that allows us to think about the future, that allowed us to identify what might endanger us there, did not follow through and take steps to avert the danger. How is it we evolved a feature that allowed scientists to think through the nature, causes, and consequences of global warming, and that enabled policy-makers to plan what would be necessary to avert those consequences, but that failed to stir up enough people to follow through with the plans?

Other primates have made great strides working out communal relations, developing simple tools to help with food gathering, and refining emotions that make for child nurturing—even if mating didn't get much refinement. But the brain that resulted from our ancestors' breeding experiments—the various hominids who gave way to Homo sapiens—left our other primate cousins in the dust. A big leap was wearing a hide and domesticating fire, thus stretching our habitat to include the whole world between the Polar Regions. A hide does not affect the climate it protects us from. But inhabiting the whole world does affect it, at first subtly and eventually profoundly. The effects were minor until the Industrial Revolution, when the global temperature began to inch upward.

Our ability to assess how we might be affecting the world we inhabit was even slower in developing. For a long time, it was merely theoretical. In the eighteenth century, Thomas Jefferson speculated that deforestation and agriculture helped to warm the climate. Alexander von Humboldt discovered that the deforestation of a valley in Venezuela was causing a nearby lake to dry up, and he wrote this observation to his correspondent, Thomas Jefferson. In 1824 Joseph Fourier first theorized the retention of solar heat in the atmosphere that would later be known as the greenhouse effect; it was first measured at the end of the nineteenth century. In the twentieth century, we dramatically sharpened our ability to measure the rise in average atmospheric temperature over time and the levels of carbon dioxide and other gases in the atmosphere now and in the past. Improvements in spectrography—the identification and measurement of chemical compounds using the way they affect light—have contributed much to this ability. So have deep core sampling in polar and other regions and improvements in measuring techniques across the sciences. In the last decades, the climate change picture became clearer when it was disentangled from the science of periodic ice age returns, which also became more precise. Current climate science is the result of interaction among many separate sciences: atmospheric physics, chemistry, astronomy, geology, computer science, mathematics. Many of these collaborate in modeling large-scale climate change over time, as well as monitoring current global temperature. After decades of debate, consensus began to form in the 1980s about the extent of global warming and its relation to the emission of carbon dioxide and other "greenhouse gases," that is, gases that contribute to absorption and retention of solar heat in the atmosphere.

Once the problem of a dangerous global rise in temperature had been identified, it became clearer what some of the obstacles to saving the planet were going to be. An effective effort would have involved an enormous cooperative push. The planning alone for real action would have taken formidable resolve. We cannot easily imagine enough agreement among nations to make a start in naming an executive committee or in designating a Greenhouse Czar. Implementation would have been more difficult by magnitudes. Poor countries unable to provide subsistence for their populations are not crazy about improving living conditions for everyone else first. Countries with plenty of resources suspect they will lose power or economic advantage by slowing production or otherwise limiting themselves.

The Paris Accord, signed in 2016, illustrates the problems of anything approaching pan-global resolve on limiting human-caused climate change. "The Paris Agreement" or "Accord de Paris" looks impressive at first glance. There are 197 countries that have signed on to the agreement. The goal is to keep the global rise in temperature below two degrees Celsius above preindustrial levels and to aim for an even lower threshold. Each country is charged with developing its own plan to aid in this effort, with reporting its progress, and with revising its plan to include more stringent measures over time.

But the agreement has all the force of a New Year's resolution. Its completely voluntary nationally determined contributions, or NDCs, even if they were adhered to, would not reach the goal of limiting the global rise in temperature to two degrees Celsius (Sophie Yeo, "Timeline: the Paris Agreement's 'Ratchet Mechanism', *Carbon Brief,* 19 January 2016). More ominously, predictions now say two degrees probably would not do the trick, anyway, and that when the earth reaches this mark (it is currently at 1.3 degrees Celsius above preindustrial levels), it may well continue warming, even if all emissions are stopped, in the beginnings of a runaway greenhouse effect (Joeri Rogelj, Michel den Elzen, Niklas Höhne, and others, "Paris Agreement Climate Proposals Need a Boost to Keep Warming Well Below 2 °C," *Nature* 534: 7609, 30 June 2016, 631–639). An extreme case of the runaway greenhouse effect is the planet Venus, which once had water oceans that have boiled off as the atmospheric carbon dioxide grew to 96% and the surface temperature climbed to a toasty 860 degrees Fahrenheit. Volcanic action tipped Venus's atmosphere into a state so rich in carbon dioxide that its heating became a self-reinforcing phenomenon. Earth does not have enough volcanic action to cause runaway heating, but humans are providing the carbon dioxide and other greenhouse gases to destroy an atmosphere that has been ideal for life for billions of years.

The magnitude of the system being disrupted makes for difficulty in grasping it. How could human beings affect something as large as Earth's atmosphere? The short answer is by sending forty billion metric tons of carbon dioxide into it each year ("There Is Still No Room for Complacency in Matters Climatic," *The Economist*, 21 September 2017). Many people say they do not believe we can have such an effect. It will be useful to tease out lack of belief on ideological or religious grounds from willful ignorance or disingenuously feigned disbelief with economic or political motives. Other actors, usually national, say that regardless of the facts they cannot or will not act to limit carbon emissions for reasons of survival or fear of the loss of political or economic hegemony.

Do some people resist acting to limit climate change from a disinterested belief or ideology untouched by self-interest? Certainly there are those people who believe it is not the public business to change the relation between humans and nature. Genesis 1:28 says "Be fruitful, and multiply, and replenish the earth, and subdue it: and have dominion over the fish of the sea, and over the fowl of the air, and over every living thing that moveth upon the earth." To a believer in the inerrancy of the Bible, such passages may underlie resistance to any idea that human "dominion" can be otherwise than God's plan. Moreover, some evangelicals believe the idea of human-caused climate change contradicts their faith in God's omnipotence ("Why So Many White Evangelicals in Trump's Base Are Deeply Skeptical of Climate Change," *The Washington Post*, Sarah Pulliam Bailey, 2 June 2017). Some conservatives and libertarians oppose government intervention for any purpose other than national defense, narrowly defined. A national and international threat of an environmental kind does not qualify as justification for these ideologues.

But most of the resistance to doing something about climate change is not disinterested, but disingenuous. The coal industry and the oil companies lobby hard against any government limitation on carbon emissions, and they have been successful in preventing any emissions trading plan, in which polluting entities such as coal-burning plants are given a cap on the amount of carbon they may emit; in such a plan they may trade carbon credits with other entities. Such emissions trading schemes, sometimes called cap and trade, are generally accepted among developed nations to be the most effective and least autocratic way to reduce carbon discharge into the atmosphere. Emissions trading laws govern carbon output in Japan, in the European Union, and elsewhere, but are not federal policy in the United States.

The resistance in the United States to the reality of climate change goes beyond lobbying and includes large-scale misinformation and propaganda campaigns funded by corporations, conservative and libertarian organizations, and evangelical Christians. These campaigns are reminiscent of the way the tobacco industry tried to discredit the science that exposed the carcinogens in all tobacco products and the huge toll in lung cancer deaths caused by cigarette use. (Robert J. Brulle, "Institutionalizing Delay: Foundation Funding and the Creation of U. S. Climate Change Counter-Movement Organizations," *Climatic Change* 122:4, 21 December 2013). Robert Brulle and others have been watching the climate change denier groups for two decades and have highlighted their methods of misinformation, cherry-picking data, and even ad hominem attacks on scientists. Recently some high-profile groups such as ExxonMobil and the Koch organization have stopped publicly supporting the climate change denial efforts, while many large donors have gone underground and now give their support through third party "pass-through" foundations (Graham Readfearn, "Climate Advocates Underestimate Power of Fossil Fueled Misinformation Campaigns," *Desmog*, 18 January 2019). A good overview of organized climate change denial in America, the role of evangelicals, conservatives, libertarians, and the Tea Party Movement, the importance of big money, and the legislative members who have figured in denial up to 2014 may be found in Jean-Daniel Collomb, "The Ideology of Climate Change Denial in the United States," *European Journal of American Studies* 9-1: Spring 2014. Social media are implicated in the propaganda campaign, since misinformation spreads fastest there.

In addition to the success of the fossil fuel lobbyists' campaign in Washington, the propaganda effort has been successful in creating some doubt among Americans about the reality of climate change. The result has been a delay in the building of a national consensus to force action on climate change mitigation. When that consensus forms, it will be too late: we will be behind the curve of self-sustaining temperature rise in the atmosphere, the first indication of runaway greenhouse effect.

To return to the question with which I began—why didn't our big brains save us?—the premise on which it is based is that big brains produce rational action, and that the evolutionary advantage that large brains with large forebrains provide should be spurring concerted action in everyone who happens to have one. But thinking about the evolution of the big brain in humans increasingly has moved toward assigning it a social rather than a purely analytical function. "The balance of evidence now clearly favors" the view that the "demands of living in large, complex societies... selected for large brains" (R. I. M. Dunbar and Susanne Shultz, "Evolution in the Social Brain," *Science* 317:5843, 7 September 2007). According to Hugo Mercier and Dan Sperber in *The Enigma of Reason* (Harvard, 2017), reason evolved in order to facilitate human cooperation in activities such as hunting. It also enables individuals in the group to preserve their status and insure they are not bearing undue risk while others are freeloading.

As Steven Sloman and Philip Fernbach put it in *The Knowledge Illusion: Why We Never Think Alone* (Penguin, 2017), our big brains evolved "in a world ruled by the logic of action" and we think in order "to choose the most effective action given the current situation" (48). For short-term decision making, we use mental shortcuts that enable quick action: detecting danger in a situation or hostility in a stranger, locating a sudden sound in our environment, moving out of the way of a falling branch or rock, braking a car or swerving to avoid an obstacle. These are individual decisions and actions. But where a decision involves action over time, with an outcome in the middle term or especially the far future, the individual is likely to revert to groupthink modality. Sloman and Fernbach think the evolutionary push favored humans who could work together in hunting, and later, building projects. They argue that "the mind...did not evolve in the context of individuals sitting alone solving problems. It evolved in the context of group collaboration, and our thinking evolved interdependently" (111). Why then did humans not get together in an enormous collaboration of everyone on earth who could help to solve the most serious global problem that has faced us?

The scope of the problem has determined the difficulties of meeting it. A problem attacking a village or a tribe, Sloman and other sources assure us, would call forth a concerted effort to solve it, with everyone acting to complement and reinforce a kind of group mind. But the climate change problem transcends tribal boundaries, regional boundaries, and national boundaries. All of the engines that drive difference rather than commonality are fired up when we attempt to solve a global problem. What are the examples that come to mind when we think of huge successful common efforts to solve a problem? The Manhattan Project? Winning the Second World War? Getting a man on the moon? I, at least, think of these three efforts that involve war or nationalistic goals before I think of one of peaceful cooperation across national lines, such as the global effort to eliminate poliomyelitis. And efforts to wipe out polio or malaria or measles do not incite the ire and resistance of corporate or national groups.

The developed nations that are autocratic such as Russia and China look at the question of limiting carbon emission in the context of global power and how such limitations would affect them as players on that stage. For democratic nations, domestic politics determine such decisions. Eventually, when large portions of America's east and west coasts are under water and when corresponding devastation faces Asia, a very probable groundswell of public outrage that borders on revolution will compel public officials to implement climate change mitigation. But I repeat: by that time the world will be facing a self-sustaining temperature rise followed by the near certainty of the runaway greenhouse effect.

The evolution of the brain created paradoxes that are revealed by the climate change crisis, since it enabled humans to identify the problem and formulate solutions but has not helped in the area of political will. In fact, it may not be too far off the mark to say the evolved brain is a political adaptation that allows large social entities to function without the friction that once led to bloodshed and tribal schism. Existing social entities get continual lubrication and maintenance from big brainers, but the big brainers are slow to form social entities that transcend tribal or national boundaries—The League of Nations, The United Nations— and slower to the point of immovability in giving such transnational groups the power to enforce any resolution or accord (the very terms indicate these agreements have little force beyond mere velleities). Moreover, the promises that the internet seemed to offer of global intelligence and powerful crowd sourcing have proved empty ones. The unity that social media delivered became merely the solipsism of disparate groups closing in on themselves. And this is where we are now.

Just a Note in Haste

Back in the day when we wrote letters to each other (with a pen or a typewriter or, in that odd transition time, writing on a computer, printing out the letter, and sending it through the mail), I remember more than one correspondent signing off with "in haste"above his signature. Virginia Woolf, reviewing some newly-found letters of Horace Walpole (1717-1797), whose correspondence would eventually fill 48 volumes in the Yale edition, says that he often used some variation of "in a violent hurry" at the beginning or end of his letters. A whole bookful of Patrick Leigh Fermor's letters exchanged with the Duchess of Devonshire was titled by its editor *In Tearing Haste*, because of the ubiquity of that phrase in Leigh Fermor's letters—though from their length and the care with which he composed them, you would not have thought him in a hurry.

No one writing an email or a text these days bothers to put down that she is in a hurry. When messages fly from writer to receiver at the speed of light ("twelve million miles a minute and that's the fastest speed there is" according to Eric Idle and Clint Black), saying she's in a hurry is superfluous. The medium *is* the message about speed here. Yet she still underlines her haste by skipping capitalization and punctuation, while abbreviating to the point of indecipherability. but u no im just :) 2 hear from her.

Almost Enough Caviar

"I was perhaps twenty-three when I first ate almost enough caviar."
– M. F. K. Fisher, *With Bold Knife and Fork*

I. The Savory Science

Sitting in the grill room of the Savoy Hotel in July, 1990, with a plate of salmon with sorrel sauce before me, I indulged in a peculiar fantasy. I imagined the sous-chef who prepared the sauce moving from the veal stock pot to the stove, adding the puréed sorrel and some cream just as he had been taught by the sous-chef before him in the same kitchen, and back and back through successive chefs and trainers of chefs to Auguste Escoffier himself, who organized and simplified the Savoy kitchens when he went there with César Ritz in 1890. From hand to hand, saucepan to stock pot to stove, there was a connection between my forkful of savory sauced fish and the hand of the great man himself a hundred years before.

This conceit was not original; I stole it, with some changes, from A. J. Liebling, whose descriptions of Paris meals eaten in the thirties can still evoke the musty, pungent aroma of truffles and cause an involuntary squirt of saliva under my tongue. Leibling was also a noted writer on boxing. He begins *The Sweet Science* by tracing his own pugilistic lineage back to the renowned boxers of the nineteenth century such as Gentleman Jim Corbett and John L. Sullivan:

> It is through Jack O'Brien ... that I trace my rapport with the historic past through the laying-on of hands. He hit me, for pedagogical example, and he had been hit by the great Bob Fitzsimmons ... Jack had a scar to show for it. Fitzsimmons had been hit by Corbett, Corbett by John L. Sullivan, he by Paddy Ryan ... and Ryan by Joe Goss, his predecessor, who

as a young man had felt the fist of the great Jem
Mace. It is a great thrill to feel that all that separates
you from the early Victorians is a series of punches
on the nose.

No more fanciful, I believe, was the connection I felt with
the gastronomic past and the great chef Auguste Escoffier as
I sat at the Savoy Hotel eating salmon with sorrel sauce. The
veal stock itself was of course one of Escoffier's tremendous
innovations in food preparation, while the nouvelle version
of the sorrel sauce made famous by the Troisgros brothers
uses no veal stock. My meal was a history lesson much more
pleasant than a punch on the nose.

That I could make such a connection, though, between
the people who had just prepared the meal I was eating in
a quiet dining room off the Strand in London and the man
who codified classic French cooking, meant that I had come
a long way.

II. Growing Up Hungry

I did not have a food-aware childhood. My mother was a
widow supporting three kids on a nurse's salary, and she
lacked the time, the money, and perhaps the imagination to
get past hot dogs and sauerkraut, Spam and baked beans,
or a dish we called goulash: she would brown a pound of
hamburger, sprinkle flour onto it until the grease was
absorbed, then add some water from the pot where she had
boiled a couple of cut-up potatoes. She heated and stirred
the meat, flour, and water until a gravy formed, dumped
in the potatoes and a can of peas, added a little salt, some
thyme, and some oregano, and it was dinner.

My food awareness changed in my early adolescence
when my mother remarried. My new stepfather was a doctor,
and though my mother worked for a while as his nurse
receptionist, eventually she was free to think about furnishing
fancy houses and entertaining guests. My stepfather liked to
cook and encouraged my mother to try interesting recipes.
Also, we often traveled on vacation to foody towns like San

Francisco and New Orleans, always eating in good restaurants. My tastes, very unschooled at first, gradually began to widen. During a whole year my restaurant meal choice was a shrimp cocktail followed by whatever sort of skewered beef the place featured. Eventually I would discover the sauces, and I can still remember my astonishment at the dish Brennan's called Eggs Hussarde, with its brown and hearty marchand de vin sauce *and* its delicate hollandaise. My parents registered my pleasure and steered me toward other sauces: mornay and other varieties of béchamel with fresh fish (another novelty to my Arizona-bred palate), beef and chasseur sauce, with its minced mushrooms, shallots, and parsley. When I discovered béarnaise, that became my choice at every restaurant that served it, with whatever they wanted to put it on.

By the time I went to college I had developed enough taste discrimination that I could not stand to eat in the school cafeteria for more than a couple of days together; since I had a meal ticket this made for budget problems when I wanted to eat in restaurants. As Jonathan Lehrer says "This is the power of cooking: it invents a new kind of desire." And then, in my sophomore year I went to Europe.

I wasn't prepared for the variety of foods I found when traveling, not only in moving from Germany to France to Italy to Greece and Turkey, but also the regional variety between a Milanese cutlet and a Tuscan beefsteak. And in truth I sampled very little of it, lacking the money, the languages, and the imagination to go beyond some of the simpler dishes. But what a revelation *they* were! I reveled in pasta with meat or fish sauces so complexly flavored, so savory they compelled slower eating. Late in my trip, in St. Germain-sur-Seine, the father of a friend taught me the rhythm of one bite of food, one small sip of wine, as we ate his superb *lapin au vin blanc*. "It dissolves the fat," he said. But in Italy, early on, there was one discovery after another. In Rome I ordered a plate of spaghetti *alla vongole* at a waiter's recommendation (though neither of us understood the other's language—and the menu had no translations) and found with surprise that the excellent sauce was filled with tender clams. Like Henry James some time before, I was pleased, surprised, and curious about how long all this had been going on over there. Adam Gopnik describes a similar experience as a young teenager when he and his family spent a year in Paris: that first night, he writes, "we went out for dinner and, for fifteen francs, had the best meal I had ever eaten, and most of all, nobody who lived there seemed to notice or care. The beauty and the braised trout alike were just part of life, the way we do things here."

While I was in Europe my parents moved to California. My first artichoke I ate in Huntington Beach, where my parents' apartment was in a complex across the street from artichoke fields, less than three miles from the beach itself. Here, too, I had my first taste of Sand Dabs, that delicate Pacific flat fish, usually no more than six inches long, with buttery flesh. I've never seen them in a restaurant away from the California coast. The frog's legs I ate at Le Petit Moulin in Santa Monica one Christmas vacation I would never have ordered; they were a surprise on the prix fixe dinner: tiny little joints in what must have been a classic *poulette* sauce of white wine and mushroom stock.

My next big food revelation came when I married and my wife Katharine and I moved to New Orleans in 1970. I know that my first encounter with whole Blue Crabs was in our first days there, at the lakeshore restaurant called Fitzgerald's—gone even before we left the city in 1976. Katharine waited patiently, having already finished her own dinner, while I worked slowly and awkwardly through a dozen of them. Later I learned faster techniques from the locals.

Our first batch of whole boiled crayfish came at the French Quarter apartment of Bill McCarthy, Cormac McCarthy's brother, who taught with us at Louisiana State University in New Orleans, later renamed the University of New Orleans. Pounds of heaped, steaming crayfish at the center of a newspaper-covered table, with bowls of red beans and rice on the side, and a technique considerably simpler than that for Blue Crabs: pull off the head and suck its juices;

put a thumb on each side of the projecting tail shell from the bottom and push with the fingers, cracking the tail open. Learning the speedy separation of a crayfish tail from its shell gives almost as much pleasure as eating the little morsels.

Where did I have my first oyster? I can't recall, but when Katharine and I moved to New Orleans in 1970 I had already developed a taste for them, and sometimes made a lunch of a couple of dozen with saltines and a Jax beer—made down on Decatur Street until the brewery was closed in our third year in town. I often went on oyster hops, eating two or three dozen at several places such as the Acme, Felix's across the street, and the Desire Oyster Bar on Bourbon. As I have said, one can make a meal of two dozen oysters, eight or ten soda crackers, and a couple of beers that will now have to be Dixie, since the Jax brewery is closed. I have eaten eight or nine dozen without feeling I had overdone it.

Another life-changing food experience was our first trip to Spain in 1983. I started keeping a journal during this trip. Katharine and I took a swing north from Madrid through León, Cantabria and the Rioja and then back to Madrid. Later we were joined by three close friends for a drive down through La Mancha to Jaén and then on to Córdoba, Seville, Granada and the Mediterranean coast. My journal records sightseeing, but it mostly talks about what we ate. And the meals were worth recording. It was my first exposure to many foods: my first baby eels, eaten as a first course for lunch in the basement *comedor* of the Alfonso XIII Hotel in Seville (eels Bilbao, with garlic and a trace of peppers), my first suckling pig, at Botín in Madrid, a restaurant famous for the dish. At El Caballo Rojo in Córdoba I had my first taste of the meaty vegetable from the thistle plant, cardos, or *cardoons* in English. Cardos are the bottoms of the European wild thistle, *Cynara cardunculus*, like a miniature artichoke heart, sweet and tender, served in this case in a cream sauce flavored with *jamón serrano*. "Cardoons with ham's cream" was the quaint translation on the menu for the English-only speaker. *Cardoons* sounds distinctly Scotch, and I suppose Scotland is known for its thistles, but the cultivated cardunculus is a southern European phenomenon. Other foods that I had disdained before, I found prepared in magical ways on this trip. The homely eggplant in the hands of a cook in Almagro became a savory appetizer; elsewhere, prepared with ham or with cheese it had inspired the sixteenth-century poet Baltasar del Alcázar to sing its praises. Spinach, never a favorite of mine, was transformed by sautéing with a little olive oil and pine nuts into a delicious side dish. In a *marisquería* in Madrid's tapas zone around the Plaza Victoria my friend David Earnest introduced me to *percebes*, goose barnacles, steamed and requiring a fair amount of unwrapping of tough hide to get to the tender meat, juicy, salty, and with the slightest hint of iodine. The many novel tastes overwhelmed the other novelties of this trip.

III. Julia

Before I came back from my trip to Europe in my college years, Julia Child was already starting to make an impact. She changed my tastes as she changed many Americans' tastes, though the process probably took ten years or more after the publication of *Mastering the Art of French Cooking*. My friends and I are all children of Julia. I was nineteen when she began her television program on WGBH, and I watched it when I could, but the book she did with Simone Beck and Louisette Bertholle was the place where I and my friends learned about shallots and lemon zest and copper pans for egg whites; we didn't always make the complicated four-page preparations, but we let her teach us about techniques and above all about appreciation. She made us into skeptics who asked, when we were reading *The Joy of Cooking* or Fannie Farmer, "does it really need to cook that long?" But I don't remember watching any other cooking program except perhaps a few episodes of *The Frugal Gourmet* when I was in graduate school. Up until I read Bill Buford's *New Yorker* article on TV cooking shows ("TV Dinners: The Rise of Food Television," October 2, 2006), it had puzzled me why I and most of my friends don't watch more of them.

According to Buford, there is already an "old days" era in food shows, epitomized by Julia Child, who clearly made food a draw for television in the first place, but who is now seen as old-fashioned. Buford has a curious take on the revolution Child created: he thinks she came off as an amateur who wasn't really sure of herself, while those of us who actually watched those shows know that it was a combination of her mastery of technique and her supreme self-confidence that enabled her to convince us that we could do that—make that omelet or pick up that dropped chicken and go on with that coq au vin.

Modern food shows are replete with what the food network executives Buford interviewed call "television values"—not an oxymoron but a matter of lighting, close-ups of food with the camera always subtly moving, audiences filmed during the lunch hour before they've eaten to prime them with hungry reactions, and personalities whose actual knowledge of cooking is deliberately upstaged by their energy or sexiness. These shows go for the lowest common denominator—the casual viewer who knows nothing about cooking—and they direct that viewer to assemble rather than to cook, taking advantage of the already peeled, cut up, and even cooked ingredients every large supermarket now carries. These shows don't have anything to teach us, whereas the "old-fashioned" ones, especially Julia's, did.

It's different with cookbooks. Here the problem is so many. Jane Kramer says there are more cookbooks published than novels or self-help books. She thinks that American women became so crazy about cookbooks because "they left their mothers behind in Europe" and weren't taught in the kitchen the cooking secrets that came down through generations. In our house, aside from Julia, we use Charlotte Walker on seafood, Penelope Casas on Spanish food as well as the Ortegas' *1080 Recipes*, now in an English translation, my old copy of Myra Waldo's *Cook as the Romans Do*, and a few others. But now we mostly learn from each other and from restaurants.

IV. Eating My Friends

When my wife and I moved to the little west Kentucky town where I taught for many years, there were no good local restaurants. There was a decent steakhouse ten miles away where one could bring a bottle of wine in. I should explain that the county, like many others in Kentucky, was dry—meaning that no liquor was sold in stores or restaurants. The law has since changed, and restaurants in town can sell liquor by the glass, and there are even package sales. The restaurants, as a result of this change, are getting better. We were lucky in finding friends who liked to cook.

At Charlotte Foreman's house we might be served Chinese chicken salad. To cooked chicken on shredded lettuce with lots of beni shoga (red pickled ginger), she added a dressing of soy, salad oil, sesame oil, rice vinegar, and a little sugar and dried mustard. She always topped the salad with mai fun (thin rice) noodles she'd just fried.

These days at David Earnest's, dinner is likely to be something out of the ordinary like anticuchos—marinated beef heart seasoned with fiery peppers and cooked on the grill. When we first came to town, it might have been a recipe from graduate school days, like the simple one-dish meal David called lime beef. He would cover ground beef with lime juice for a few hours. Then he'd sauté garlic cloves, green onions, and chopped serrano peppers with the beef, throw in coarsely chopped Bok Choy, sprinkle everything with soy sauce, cover it up and steam it for a few minutes.

Another bachelor friend, Richard Steiger, makes a specialty of roasted chicken, which he prepares in various ways. Charlotte Beahan, who teaches Chinese history, makes *jao-tze*, delicious steamed pork dumplings. Pam Cartwright serves a low-country breakfast dish of shrimp and grits.

When my wife and I invited people in, we often served them the flank steak that our old friend Cynthia Doster showed us how to prepare. She marinates the flank steak in equal portions of oil and lemon juice (with the lemon's zest) and soy sauce, adds a healthy dose of minced garlic, a teaspoon of brown sugar, and—the heart of the marinade—a teaspoon of fresh ginger. This dish remained a staple in our household even after the price of flank steak—very cheap in our graduate school days—rose to rival that of the tenderer beef varieties. We grill the meat on a barbecue cooker until just past rare, slice it into thin strips, and almost always serve it with twice-baked potatoes.

We might begin with an appetizer of ceviche. Pat Kent, my oldest friend, dead now these many years, showed me the simplest and best ceviche preparation I know of. He put bay scallops in lime juice for 24 hours, drained them, and added *pico de gallo*—chopped fresh tomatoes, serrano or jalapeño peppers, onions, and cilantro. Bay scallops, smaller than sea scallops, are just the right size to be cooked through by the lime juice in a day. I add some olive oil along with the salsa, and of course, salt.

V. Don't Try This at Home

My friend David Earnest has a habit of saying about a dish he's enjoying at a restaurant, "We could do this." Of course, we all get ideas from restaurant preparations. At the Brasserie Le Coze in Atlanta, I was served a salad of Belgian Endive with a mixture spooned onto the leaves consisting of some of the endive centers chopped with Roquefort and a little vinaigrette dressing. Unlike some dishes, its ingredients and preparation were obvious, and I now serve this endive dish as an appetizer and a salad. But my ordinary reaction to a good restaurant dish is just to enjoy it. The restaurant experience, for me, is partly the pleasure of having someone else prepare the food (and wash the dishes). Moreover, I like to think of each restaurant as the place where a favorite dish lives, a place I must visit in order to enjoy the black ravioli stuffed with lobster (Nais Cuisine in Havertown, Pennsylvania), or the oysters marinated in lemon juice and served with chopped endive and spoonfish caviar (Maisonnette in Cincinnatti, which, alas, I can visit only in memory). The conviction that the taste remains attached to the place is even stronger for those dishes served in restaurants in Spain or France or Italy.

My stepfather and mother also suffered from the knowledge that they could prepare a restaurant dish they liked, and I can see them analyzing as they chewed, even before one asked, "Is that tarragon?" or "Did they use asiago in that?" I can hear my stepfather asking, "Why should I pay twenty-five dollars for a dish I can make myself at home for five?" There is no answer to this question, once it has been said aloud. A restaurant meal for me is not a regrettably expensive substitute for eating at home.

"Going out," we call it, and it *is* out of the everyday and domestic and into the world. We break the routine and seek novelty, even when the restaurant is well-known to us. Even at the familiar restaurant, which we may love because of its consistency, there is the possibility of surprise, of "the special." Dining out has an element of travel, of visiting new spots or revisiting favorite old ones.

VI. A Clean, Well-lighted Place

I made a list of a dozen wonderful restaurants where I have eaten and found another element in restaurant dining: the ephemeral. Here is my list:

> Beijing in Vancouver
> Nais Cuisine in Havertown, PA
> Monti's La Casa Vieja in Tempe, Arizona
> Le Petit Moulin in Santa Monica
> Maisonette in Cincinnatti
> Mario's in Nashville
> Le Midi in Charleston, South Carolina
> La Mer à Boire in Montreal
> Brasserie Le Coze in Atlanta
> Le Bistro in Tucson
> Le Bec Fin in Philadelphia
> Le Ruth's in New Orleans

A random list of favorites scattered around the continent rather than a "top dozen" or otherwise ranked or categorized list, this group of restaurants includes only places where I have eaten more than once. Le Bistro in Tucson was almost a neighborhood restaurant for me and my wife, a regular weekly stop. But no more. When I first published this essay in 2014, only the first three restaurants on this list were still going; at the moment, only one, Beijing in Vancouver, still exists.

A talk show I watched in New Orleans in the 70s featured managers and owners of top local restaurants. Warren Le Ruth was there with managers from Antoine's, Arnaud's, and Commander's Palace (this was before Emeril LeGasse had his own restaurant). One of the comments I remember was the statistic that less than ten percent of new restaurants are still open after a year in the same place, and less than five percent are still under the same ownership. The fearful attrition of even successful, established restaurants (all the ones on my list were going concerns) suggests that recalling any good restaurant meal is indulging in elegy, and unashamedly that is what I am doing here.

At Maisonette—which Mobil gave five stars for more years than any other restaurant—I might begin with a glass of Bollinger or Roederer or Entre Deux Mers with a leek and potato soup or an appetizer of ravioli stuffed with artichokes and arugula, with a sauce of tomato and arugula oil. The main course could be monkfish on a mousse of chervil and dill with a little crabmeat, or the rack of lamb, or brill and Florida lobster in puff pastry with a butter sauce. With the fish I would be drinking a Bernardus Chardonnay or a Pouilly Fuissé; with the lamb a glass of St. Francis Cabernet. The *crème brulée* was always good, but I preferred the combinations of white and dark chocolate mousse with various sauces.

Mario's, where my wife and I often celebrated our anniversaries, burned in 2007 and has not rebuilt. Though not a very imaginative restaurant, Mario's could produce wonderful manifestations of traditional dishes, and I remember with great fondness an appetizer special of crabmeat ravioli with a champagne cream sauce.

Le Ruth's was New Orleans' best restaurant (though not even in the city but across the river in Algiers) in the early seventies when the competition was stiff. Two dishes they did exceptionally well were the oyster and artichoke soup—the best example of this common New Orleans dish—and a sole rolled around an oyster and crab stuffing. Le Ruth's almond torte was also a stunner.

Le Midi was only briefly alive in Charleston, but I managed three visits there during two convention trips. It was a small bistro that served provincial French cooking. La Mer à Boire in Montreal served the best snails I've ever eaten, in little pastry shells and caps with a superb brown sauce. The strange thing about the disappearance of this restaurant is that though you will not find La Mer à Boire, you will find a microbrewery with a similar name. *La mer à boire*—"the whole ocean to drink"—means a difficult task and is usually used in the negative: "*Ce n'est pas la mer à boire.*" The brew pub's name puns on the idomatic expression and turns it into "L'Amere à boire"—the bitter (beer) to drink.

VII. Eating to Live, Living to Eat

Of the important things in life, people, books, and food, food is perhaps the least important. But this simple separation ignores the connections and parallels. Like the book, food has a double life. Books are commodities that can be bought or sold as well as repositories of ideas that can alter the world. Food is also a commodity, one that exists only to be consumed—the ultimate commodity of a consumer culture. But its material aspect shades off into the nonmaterial in its aesthetic and social roles. Food can be art that satisfies sight with color and contrast, satisfies touch with texture and tastes of a hundred thousand subtleties. Food's material presence literally sustains us; it is fuel. It is also idea: through the senses it excites the mind.

The social aspect of food is a distinguishing feature. True, I can remember the surroundings when and where I first read Saroyan and Joyce and the New Testament, but the people around me at the time are not a notable part of the memory. Reading usually substitutes its own world for the one surrounding the reader instead of heightening one's awareness of that surrounding world. Books are isolating in this respect; food brings people together and makes them remember the place, the time, the company. Bulwer-Lytton was simply wrong when he wrote "we can live without friends; we can live without books, / But civilized man cannot live without cooks." Without the friends and the books, we aren't civilized, and we can't appreciate the cooks. And what we share with friends goes beyond the immediate breaking of bread: Brillat-Savarin, whose *The Physiology of Taste* has the subtitle *Meditations of Transcendent Gastronomy*, said that the last and most enjoyable sensation of food is reflection.

A friend who could not accompany us on that notable trip to Spain commented how she pictured us: "I see you all sitting at a table, eating and talking and drinking and laughing, with piles of fish bones in front of you." She was right on the mark, except that some evenings the piles were lamb bones or pig carcasses or rabbit remains. I would like to think my enjoyment of the friends, like my appreciation of the food, has refined and increased over the years.

Getting Past the ABCs

> "Eddyville Ground, this is Cessna Four Niner Romeo Papa with Information Lima at the terminal, ready for taxi."
> "Niner Romeo Papa, taxi to Runway Six Right, left on Delta, right on Charlie, left on Foxtrot, hold short of Runway Tree Tree."

When an Air Traffic Controller talks to a pilot on the radio, he uses a pronunciation of several numerals— tree (3), fife (5), and niner (9)—designed to cut through static and poor transmission, rendering confusion—between five and nine, for example—less likely. And this conversation uses the communications alphabet, also called the phonetic or radio alphabet, for clear and unambiguous radio exchanges.

Alfa	November
Bravo	Oscar
Charlie	Papa
Delta	Quebec
Echo	Romeo
Foxtrot	Sierra
Golf	Tango
Hotel	Uniform
India	Victor
Juliett	Whiskey
Kilo	Xray
Lima	Yankee
Mike	Zulu

Hundreds of such exchanges occur every day, and aviation traffic is safer because of this universally understood ABC. But as businesslike and matter-of-fact as the radio alphabet seems, a closer look shows it is packed with history, romance, mythology, literature, and the lure of faraway places.

The International Civil Aviation Organization (ICAO), an agency of the United Nations, adopted the communications alphabet in 1952. Soon NATO, our own armed forces, and the International Telecommunications Union (ITU) also adopted the alphabet. For the U. S. Army and Navy, it replaced the Able Baker Charlie Dog Easy alphabet familiar from WWII movies. *The Aeronautical Information Manual* (AIM) specifies in Chapter 4-2-7 that the ICAO phonetic alphabet be used by pilots. The version printed there is actually the ITU alphabet, which uses Alfa instead of Alpha (Spanish pilots might be tempted to say Al-pa) and Juliett instead of Juliet (so French pilots won't say Jool-ee-ay).

Although there seems to be a solid American base to the alphabet, with homely names like Charlie and Mike as well as the patriotic Yankee, we also get hints of the more cosmopolitan. You may be figuring weights and balance in pounds, but Kilo is a reminder that there are other measures—in Lima, for instance, or Quebec, or all over India.

As for history, Alpha and Delta are taken straight from the Greek alphabet, only a step removed from an earlier form of writing using stylized pictures, or *pictographs*. Alpha, for example, derives ultimately from the Hebrew *aleph*, which meant *ox*. Just turn the capital A upside down to see the ox's head.

Romeo and Juliet, of course, are Shakespeare's star-crossed lovers, children of two feuding families in the Italian city of Verona. In the Greek myth, Echo was the nymph who loved the self-absorbed youth Narcissus, pining away until only her voice remained. And could Papa be Hemingway?

There's a whiff of the getaway vacation in Hotel and Golf, and the alphabet suggests a taste of nightlife: have a Whiskey and dance the Foxtrot. If you can manage the more exotic Tango, you might prompt a "Bravo!" from the spectators.

So, the next time you use the familiar letters of the radio alphabet, think of its cosmopolitan cultural background. From its Greek beginnings in Alpha to the African zest of Zulu, this bunch of letters gets past the simple ABCs!

Agonists

"Perhaps I want them to wince."
—Nancy Mairs, "On Being a Cripple" (1986)

There is a group of contemporary writers whose subject is their own suffering. The ones that come to mind most readily are Nancy Mairs, Carolyn Knapp, Marjorie Williams, and Andre Dubus. Many writers have a single essay or two that would qualify—Joyce Carol Oates describing her attacks of tachycardia in "Against Nature," for example. Until she wrote *The Year of Magical Thinking* I would not have included Joan Didion here, though her 1979 essay on migraine headaches, "In Bed," was a classic description, and very reassuring to those of us who had been treated to the kinds of responses she describes: the suggestion that a couple of aspirin might be a remedy we had never thought of, or the supremely condescending, "I'd have a headache, too, spending a beautiful day like this inside with all the shades drawn." But writers such as Mairs and Knapp and Dubus make a subject of their afflictions and return to that subject. I have called them "agonists" because they seem to embody all of the original meanings of the Greek word that came down to us as *agony*: the struggle, the public contest, the anguish. These writers are performing their struggle with suffering; by writing, they make public the pain that is ordinarily invisible and always located within the single self. Three of the group I have mentioned have already lost the struggle and are dead. Nancy Mairs, who survives, is perhaps the best exemplar of the group in her concentration on her own and her family's suffering in her nonfiction writing. [Since the magazine publication of this essay, Mairs has also died.]

Reading the work of these writers leads me to ask why one reads material that is painful—though the reader's pain is hugely attenuated from that which is described. And the next question is why these writers would want to revisit their pain again by writing about it. As I read I deferred the first question and concentrated on the second, discovering in the process that there are almost as many reasons for writing about suffering as there are writers who do it.

Some Proto-agonists

It would be a mistake to suppose that the writer's focus on her or his own discomfort is somehow a modern trend. The self as subject necessarily includes the suffering self, as we can find in the work of the first essayist, Michel de Montaigne. He suffered from migraine headaches and from depression, which he fought by writing the *Essays*. "It was a melancholy humor, and consequently a humor very hostile to my natural disposition, produced by the gloom of the solitude into which I had cast myself some years ago, that first put into my head this daydream of meddling with writing." The remedy seems to have worked. But less tractable than his migraines (which seem to have lessened over the years) and his melancholy were the kidney stones that tortured him. He does not often mention his health, but in two essays he gives more space to the topic.

Montaigne feared kidney stones because they killed his father, he tells us in "Of the Resemblance of Children to Fathers." They began about 1578, when Montaigne was 45, but after more than a year of the symptoms, he found he was "already growing reconciled to this colicky life" and mused that "I had more fear of them than I have found pain in them." But it is, he conceded, "the worst of all maladies, the most sudden, the most painful," and he found its onset both sudden and severe. In "Of Experience" he talks about what one can expect from the disease: "you sweat in agony, turn pale, turn red, tremble, vomit your very blood...discharge thick, black, and frightful urine, or have it stopped up by some sharp rough stone that cruelly pricks and flays the neck of your penis." He thinks that his illness may help reconcile him to death—"consider how artfully and gently the stone weans you from life and detaches you from the world....If you do not embrace death, at least you shake hands with it once a month." But philosophical consolations aside, he believes that we ought to be allowed to complain and to cry out in pain—that philosophy should not require more than we can humanly do. He comments ironically on the stones' effect on his sex life: "Oh, why have I not the faculty of that dreamer in Cicero who, dreaming he was embracing a wench, found that he had discharged his stone in the sheets! Mine extraordinarily diswench me." And he rhapsodizes about the euphoria that follows the passing of a stone: "But is there anything so sweet as that sudden change, when from extreme pain, by the voiding of my stone, I come to recover as if by lightning the beautiful light of health?" It is tempting to make the figurative equation of writing with voiding the stone.

The narrative of addiction is not exclusively modern, either. Charles Lamb's "Confessions of a Drunkard" was published in 1813 and may be the first description of alcoholism from the point of view of the alcoholic. Lamb says there is a "constitutional tendency" to drunkenness and "when a man has commenced sot" it is very hard to start reforming. He sees clearly that not everyone has the tendency. He talks about screaming at the effort of abstaining for just one day. At twenty-six, he began drinking excessively, possibly as a way of lessening his stammer. Soon he has to drink until he becomes drunk: "In my stage of habit...to stop short of that measure which is sufficient to draw on torpor and sleep, the benumbing apoplectic sleep of the drunkard, is to have taken none at all." And he insists that once one has arrived at this state, "reason shall only visit him through intoxication...The drinking man is never less himself than during his sober intervals."

He talks about the abulia consequent upon habitual drinking: "any small duty...haunts me as a labour impossible to be got through. So much the springs of action are broken." His powers of concentration are gone: "This poor abstract of my condition was penned at long intervals, with scarcely any attempt at connection of thought, which is now difficult to me." This assertion of lost powers is perhaps disingenuous, since many a sober essay writer begins with disconnected pieces.

Lamb's careful anatomizing of his disease has led many of his defenders to deny that he was really an alcoholic and to insist on the writer's license to exaggerate. These sympathetic critics are made uncomfortable by thinking of their man in the state he describes. It makes them wince. We cannot settle this question from the distance of two centuries, but we know for certain that when it comes to misfortune and suffering, Lamb's plate was full. Nowhere in his essays does he mention his taking on, at the age of twenty-one, the complete care of his sister, who in a fit of insanity killed their mother, or his continuing care of her until his own death—care which included attentive watching for signs of her mania recurring. Lamb's biographer Barry Cornwall reported that when Lamb saw such signs in Mary, "he would take her under his arm to Hoxton Asylum. It was very affecting to encounter the young brother and sister walking together (weeping) on this painful errand, Mary herself, although sad, very conscious of the necessity of a temporary separation from her only friend. They used to carry a strait waistcoat with them." Nor does Lamb mention that he himself spent six weeks in a psychiatric hospital in 1795, a few months before Mary's murderous outbreak. His avoiding any writing about Mary raises a question about boundaries: does Lamb think his own suffering is a reasonable subject, but that his sister's is off limits?

Thomas De Quincey writes about his opium addiction in "Confessions of an English Opium-Eater," published in 1821. He began using opium for a stomach problem, carefully keeping the dose to about twenty-five drops of the tincture of opium called laudanum. He used opium in this way over an eight-year period from 1804 to 1812, without any real ill effects. It was a "recreational drug" according to the modern expression, and he used it on Saturday evenings and then went rambling through the city observing the behavior of his fellow citizens and being entertained by it. He argues that in such dosages it doesn't produce the effects of torpor and inactivity that some ascribe to it. An illness in 1813 was the occasion for his beginning to take the drug daily, in a greatly increased dose. By 1817 he was experiencing intellectual paralysis, and he describes the melancholy and the vivid nightmares he had every time he slept, involving distortions of space and time, oppressive architecture, expanses of water, "Asiatic" low-life scenes, threatening animals, and other horrors. The nightmares got worse whenever he tried to lessen the amount of opium he was taking, which at its height was about eight thousand drops of laudanum, per day—the equivalent of about eighty teaspoons, containing about 320 grains of opium. At length he realized that he was going to die if he continued to take opium, so he resolved that if he must die either way, he would die in the attempt to stop, and he managed to stop, though his dreams were still tormented at the time of writing the essay, many months after leaving off any use of the drug.

Knapp, Williams, and Dubus

Among modern writers on the subject of addiction, one of the most prolific has been Caroline Knapp. Knapp's first book was *Drinking: A Love Story* (1996). She was born in 1960 and died in 2002 of lung cancer. She does not talk about smoking in this book or in *Appetites: Why Women Want* (2003), a book about her struggle with anorexia, published after her death. Her columns with the byline "Alice K" were collected as *Alice K.'s Guide to Life: One Woman's Quest for Survival, Sanity and the Perfect New Shoes* (1994). *The Merry Recluse: A Life in Essays* (2004) is a group of Caroline Knapp's essays put together by Sandra Shea, who was Knapp's editor at the *Boston Phoenix*. Knapp might not have chosen that particular essay, the last here, for the collection title, but much of her writing in her *Boston Phoenix* columns under the byline "Alice K" was funny. "Dicking Around" explores the question of why "the average man has 27 names for his dick, while "women are much more discreet about their reproductive anatomy." "What Women Really Need from Science" suggests there are a lot of things science could do more useful to women than fixing things so women at advanced ages can have babies. Knapp's point of view is always very personal, centered in her own experience and her own gender.

Not funny are the essays about Knapp's alcoholism and recovery from it, about her anorexia and recovery from it, about her solitude and very complicated feelings about it, about her (fraternal) twin sister, about her father and mother and their deaths and her grieving. She is convincing about how addiction anesthetizes her against the world and how she does not grow and progress because real decisions are deferred. "People in drinking-and-recovery circles often say that...you stop growing when you start drinking alcoholically." She provides careful, clinical, detailed self-observation about both her eating disorder and her alcoholism.

Knapp's approach to her own suffering is journalistic. Lamb and De Quincey are both aware that there is a sensational element to the descriptions they give of their descent into addiction. With Knapp one has the feeling she is merely trying to get it right, and that the success in detailing symptoms and progress justifies the effort of recalling them.

Marjorie Williams writes not about addiction but about her own deadly disease. Williams wrote not-very-flattering political profiles (of Vernon Jordan and Barbara Bush, for examples) that appeared in *Vanity Fair* and the *Washington Post*, but most of her pieces, both political and personal, appeared in the *Post*. A few were unpublished at the time of her death, including "The Alchemist," an appreciation of her mother, who gave up a career as a chemist to become a housewife, turned herself into a gourmet cook, and drank herself to death at the age of seventy. Williams sees her mother using food to distance herself: "You could eat at her table every night and never once taste the thing you were really hungry for." *The Woman at the Washington Zoo: Writings on Politics, Family, and Fate*, edited by Timothy Noah (2005), is a posthumous collection of Marjorie Williams's writings collected by her husband after her death from liver cancer in 2005.

Marjorie Williams was diagnosed with metastatic stage IV(b) liver cancer in July, 2001. "There is no V, and there is no (c)," she writes in "Hit by Lightning: A Cancer Memoir," another previously unpublished essay, which takes us almost three years into the disease that was supposed to have killed her within six months.

Williams's writing about her cancer and her life after her diagnosis strikes me as having a very specific target audience: she is leaving behind an account her children will be able to understand when they are grown; she is talking to them as adults, as she will be unable to do in any other way. The key essay here, in which she tells us her children are eight and six years old, is "Telling the Real, Real Truth." Here she writes about her children's pressing her about whether Santa is just a fiction (with the subtext about whether she is telling them the truth about her cancer). Elsewhere she describes their puzzlement over why everyone seems so exercised about another bunch of killings (the Malvo/Muhammed sniper murders in the Washington area where they live), and in a comment that is revealing about her treatment, she explains why we don't want a doctor as a president (Howard Dean was running): "Where else but in medicine do you find men and women who never admit a mistake? Who talk more than they listen, and feel entitled to withhold crucial information? Whose lack of tact in matters of life and death might disqualify them for any other field?"

In 1986, when he was 49, Andre Dubus stopped to help a hurt motorist and was struck by a passing car. It's a scene that happens with frightening frequency; my younger son was almost killed in such a situation. Dubus lost one leg and the use of the other. He was confined to a wheelchair, and, while he did not see that as a defining condition of his life, it is of many of the essays in *Broken Vessels* (1991) and *Meditations from a Movable Chair* (1998), published the year before Dubus died of a heart attack at the age of 62.

"Lights of the Long Night" is the name of the essay in *Broken Vessels* in which Dubus describes the accident that crippled him—and cripple is a word he insists on to describe himself. Although, as Tobias Wolff says in his introduction, there is "no whining" in these essays, there is painful detail to Dubus's relation of the accident, the failing of his marriage, the reaction of his older child to these events, and, in a particularly horrible moment, the cutting off of the end of his thirteen-month-old child's finger in an exercise machine while Dubus is powerless to get to her to prevent it. As Wolff writes, "Dubus has the writer's gift of subduing shock and rage and grief by translating them into meticulous observation."

The essays in the 1998 collection are less likely to make us wince. Dubus writes a letter to politicians about the difficulty of traveling on Amtrak or on airlines with his leg, which won't bend at the knee. He writes about grace and the sacramental in the ordinary and the physical. When Dubus was seventeen, his father made him take a construction job, which turned out to be digging ditches with a pick and shovel; he writes about that and about his experience on a carrier for a year, during which a friend, an airman and Air Guard Commander, killed himself when the Navy's investigators discovered he was homosexual. He describes giving up his guns when he realizes carrying one means that sooner or later he will kill someone. The essays, though not necessarily about his own body, do not stray far from the obtrusiveness of the body and from its mortality. The suffering body can be distracted by writing; the result may transcend mortality and thus the suffering body.

An Agonist Manqué

It might be helpful in considering the motivation and reception of agonist writing to consider the case of James Frey, who wrote a book exaggerating and outright inventing his own disasters. In 2003 Doubleday published Frey's book *A Million Little Pieces*. Doubleday's Anchor division reissued the book in paperback in 2005. In September, 2005, Oprah Winfrey selected Frey's book for her book club and praised it on her daytime television show. In *A Million Little Pieces*, Frey paints a picture of himself as one turned into a monster by his liquor and drug addictions. He recalls his role in a train accident that killed two of his schoolmates, talks about spending months in jail, and claims to be still wanted in several states for his crimes.

An investigative website called "The Smoking Gun," which finds and posts public documents that show when politicians and others in the public eye are lying, began to look into Frey's police records almost immediately after the Winfrey endorsement. "The Smoking Gun" discovered that Frey had invented most of the more lurid episodes in the book: he had no part in the train accident, for example, and he had not served jail time, nor was he ever a fugitive.

When "The Smoking Gun" news first broke, Larry King had Frey on his show and quizzed him about the facts. Oprah Winfrey telephoned the program to defend Frey on the air. Two weeks later she invited Frey and his publisher to her show, apologized to her audience for defending the book, and grilled Frey about its details, with tears and execrations. "I have to say it is difficult for me to talk to you because I really feel duped," she said. "I feel that you betrayed millions of readers." Frey, no doubt, was almost as eager as his publisher to go through this public auto-da-fé, which certainly increased his notoriety and probably his sales.

More surprising, perhaps, was the reaction of Lee Gutkind, who edits the magazine called *Creative Nonfiction*. Gutkind, in a 2006 issue of the magazine, writes a preface about what he calls "the Frey scandal." Gutkind rather naively assumes this episode somehow impugns the reputation of nonfiction writing, and since he conceives of the mission of his magazine to "help define and, if necessary, defend the genre," he points out that the essays in this issue also talk about difficult life experiences, adding, "and they're true."

The Oprah reaction may not be as naive as it first appears, and suggests that we all want to wince, to shift uncomfortably in our reading chairs and perhaps to cry, but we want the suffering that evokes these responses to be real. The original audiences of classical Greek tragedies and of Shakespeare's tragedies believed the stories on which the plays were based to be true. If you look at the blurbs on the cover of Joan Didion's *The Year of Magical Thinking*, you will find that the reviewers insist on the book's honesty, candor, and exactness. Looking at these blurbs, I found myself wondering how they can know the book has any of these qualities. Is it because Didion paints an unflattering picture of herself? Or is it because of our reaction that no one would make up these things, no one would write down such a combination of the horrible and the ordinary? Of course, the horrible things are a matter of public record: the death of Didion's husband, John Gregory Dunne, while their daughter was in intensive care, and the daughter's partial recovery and subsequent brain hemorrhage. But because we make some sort of equation between honesty and describing one's own suffering, the revelations of Frey's inventions and exaggerations caused such an outcry.

Joan Didion and *The Year of Writing Dangerously*

Didion writes about the year of her husband's death and the onset of her daughter's health problems. Didion's daughter, Quintana, went into the hospital on Christmas morning with what looked like a bad case of flu. Pneumonia followed, and then septic shock. Five nights after her admission, Didion's husband, John Gregory Dunne, died suddenly of a heart attack. Some weeks later Quintana, after being released from one hospital, was readmitted to another for an arterial bleed (she had been given anticoagulants for clots that formed during her long inactivity at the time of the first hospitalization). Each short respite was almost immediately followed by a new disaster.

Didion wanted to be alone on the first night after Dunne's death "so he could come back. This," she writes, "was the beginning of my year of magical thinking." For much of the year she entertained, in conscious thought but just below the level of her concentrated attention, an utterly irrational conviction that Dunne could somehow be brought back from the dead.

Didion studies the literature: C.S. Lewis's *A Grief Observed* (a journal he kept after his wife's death), Philippe Ariès' *Western Attitudes toward Death: From the Middle Ages to the Present* (1973), Geoffrey Gorer's, *Death, Grief, and Mourning* (1965), Emily Post on the etiquette of funerals (1922), articles on grief in *The Journal of the American Psychiatric Association* and *The Lancet*, a National Academy of Science Institutes of Medicine compilation on bereavement (1984). She compares her reactions to those observed by the professionals. She *works up* the topic. She understands this behavior as being, not a reaction to her grief, but her *modus operandi* as a writer. She describes herself as not being willing or able to insert herself into her writing ordinarily, yet in this case she feels the need to do so.

> This is my attempt to make sense of the period that followed, weeks and then months that cut loose any fixed idea I had ever had about death, about illness, about probability and luck, about good fortune and bad, about marriage and children and memory, about grief, about the ways in which people do and do not deal with the fact that life ends, about the shallowness of sanity, about life itself. I have been a writer my entire life. As a writer, even as a child, long before what I wrote began to be published, I developed a sense that meaning itself was resident in the rhythms of words and sentences and paragraphs, a technique for withholding whatever it was I thought or believed behind an increasingly impenetrable polish. The way I write is who I am, yet this is a case in which I wish I had instead of words and their rhythms…a digital editing system on which I could…show you simultaneously all the frames of memory…. This is a case in which I need more than words to find the meaning.

She wishes she had images instead of words, and admits that here the usual observation about the writer making sense of experience through ordering it in writing breaks down—*but she writes about it anyway.* In the end, suffering and grief are the test cases for the cliché about writers making sense of experience through ordering it, and the test is failed.

In Los Angeles, where Quintana is in a UCLA intensive care unit, Didion moves back and forth from her hotel to the hospital, trying to avoid the memory "vortex"—since they had lived in the area for many years, in Malibu and in Brentwood. And there is what she calls the "Appointment in Samarra" aspect of grief and memory: if I had been here or done that, could the disaster have been avoided?

She flies back to New York with Quintana on an ambulance plane. In New York, as her daughter starts to recover, Didion resolves to do the same. She stops trying "to substitute an alternate reel" in the summer of 2004 and begins trying to reconstruct everything leading up to Dunne's death. She talks about encountering meaninglessness and about the self-pity that seems unavoidable (when younger, she dismissed the "whining" she found in Dylan Thomas's widow Caitlin's *Leftover Life to Kill*). When she gets the autopsy report she realizes Dunne was dead instantly and no intervention or preventive measure (the angioplasty in that artery twenty years before had already taken him past normal expectations) could have changed the outcome.

She begins to write again in August and September; she has friends for dinner on Christmas Eve as they'd done the year before. "The craziness is receding," she writes, "but no clarity is taking its place."

Nancy Mairs and The Literature of Personal Disaster

Nancy Mairs was born in 1943 and lives in Tucson. She began to experience the symptoms of multiple sclerosis when she was twenty-eight. By 1986, when she was in her forties, she was walking with a cane, and by 1992, she was in a wheelchair. But it is not only the progress of her MS that she writes about. In a series of books since 1986 she has written about her depression and attempted suicide, the murder of her adopted son, her agoraphobia, and her husband's malignant melanoma. *Plaintext* came out in 1986 and includes the essay in which she discusses the onset of her MS, "On Being a Cripple." This book was followed by *Remembering the Bone House* (1989), *Carnal Acts* (1990), *Ordinary Time* (1993), *Voice Lessons: On Becoming a (Woman) Writer* (1994), *Waist High in the World* (1994), and *A Troubled Guest: Life and Death Stories* (2001).

Mairs, like Dubus, calls herself a cripple: "I am a cripple. I choose this word to name me." Part of the reason for using this word, she admits, is that she wants to be seen as tough-minded about her afflictions. This is a theme to which she returns in "The Literature of Personal Disaster," an essay in *Voice Lessons,* where she writes that victims such as herself can "write their way into better behavior than they believed themselves capable of. I am forever publishing brave statements that I must then make good on if I am to be a woman of my word." Here writing has nothing to do with transcending the experience, but instead with shaping expectations from the outside while one is living. The mode is survival rather than transcendence.

In this essay, Mairs writes at the bedside of her husband, who has metastatic melanoma. She says we imagine that we are alone in suffering, "each of us trapped in this profound and irrational solitude, as though walls of black glass had dropped on every side, shutting out the light, deadening all sound but the loved one's morphine-drugged breathing." But, she says, we are not alone, and asks whether it was "that intuition which had driven me before, and would goad me again, to write intimately about illness, disability, and death? And does the same suspicion provoke others to tell their stories—so much like mine, so absolutely their own? Are we all groping for one another through our separate darks?"

Mairs says that because she writes about these matters, she is often called upon to review and endorse works, that she calls "only half-facetiously, the Literature of Personal Disaster." She lists some works she's reviewed: Andre Dubus's *Broken Vessels*, Elizabeth Cox's *Thanksgiving: An AIDS Journal*, Kate Millet's *The Loony-Bin Trip*, May Sarton's *After the Stroke*, and others. "What do the bookmongers believe will draw readers to these?" she asks. "Sorrow? Curiosity? What are they supposed to find there? Solace? Reassurance? Sheer relief that, however wretched their own lives may seem, others are worse?"

She gives us hints about why she herself reads these books. She finds in Andre Dubus's *Broken Vessels* evidence of "the spiritual maturation that suffering can force." And in Susan Kenney's books *In Another Country* and *Sailing* she finds a revelation about the quotidian nature of suffering, "the way cancer has to fit in among children's tantrums and Christmas shopping and the pressures of work and the death of the old dog." Reading this, I was reminded of W. H. Auden finding such a revelation in Breughel paintings, as he writes in "Musée des Beaux Arts":

> About suffering they were never wrong,
> The Old Masters: how well they understood
> Its human position; how it takes place
> While someone else is eating or opening a window
> or just walking dully along....

Such writers as Kenney, according to Mairs, show "suffering in its proper scale, not inconsequential, by any means, but not insurmountable either."

She dismisses the idea of whining, saying that being a victim, really being singled out for suffering, takes work, and that the "narrator of personal disaster" wants to comfort, not to whine, and "to persuade the skeptical reader...that survival...is possible."

Is There Anything We Can Do with Suffering Except to Suffer It?

We read the accounts of people suffering for some of the same reasons we read all tragedy. The catharsis of pity and terror. The feeling of relief that it is not me. If we are sufferers ourselves, or if we have someone near to us who is, we read for the comfort of knowing we are not alone, and for the hints of coping strategy we might find.

But I don't think that authors who write about suffering are motivated primarily by their knowledge that readers want these things. An eye on the reader seems more likely to energize the James Frey type of writer. It is true that Mairs says the writer of personal disaster "wants to comfort," and the social impulse cannot be neglected. Mairs also admits that "Real readers, in fact, puzzle me a bit, the way women puzzled Freud." The reader may be the idealized reader who is the writer herself (and Mairs admits to constructing such an ideal reader), or the potential readers who are Marjorie Williams's ungrown children. I believe, as I wrote earlier, that the motives of these writers are as many and as various as the writers themselves.

A further possibility is that these people, being writers, *must* write, and their suffering is the largest thing in their field of view, so they write about it. Yet there is mystery here. Do the usual compensations apply: the illusion of control, of ordering to understand, and of getting it off the chest? "I wrote compulsively, hour after hour," Nancy Mairs reports, "as though capturing my world in detail could defer its end." The experience of Didion suggests that the effort does not make sense of the suffering, or make it better. Yet it may function to keep a hold on sanity, or to pull oneself back from dropping off its edge.

Writing exercises capacities that remain in the suffering writer. C. S. Lewis wavers on the subject of whether writing helps. He kept a notebook after his wife Helen Joy Gresham Lewis died in 1960, after four years of marriage to Lewis. The notebook was eventually published as an essay-length book. Lewis wonders whether thinking about his grief in this way might make it worse. "But what am I to do?" he asks. "By writing it all down (all?—no: one thought in a hundred) I believe I get a little outside it." He poses the question whether there is anything "we can do with suffering except to suffer it." Lewis knows that it is by no means certain suffering will be assuaged by this effort of writing, of looking at one's own reactions. Reading Lewis's *A Grief Observed*, I am reminded about Samuel Johnson's grief after his wife's death, and the way he tortures himself in his prayers (some of which he recorded) with the thought that the grief itself might be prolonged and excessive enough to be sinful. With grief, we have a special case for writing in the need to revisit the experience with that part of the mind only engaged by writing. In other words, for a writer, writing about the loved one may be as necessary to the course of grief as going through each of the seasons without the person one has lost. Until a year after John Gregory Dunne's death, and until she begins to write again, Didion talks about being "ambushed" by grief.

Writing can also be connection. Montaigne's melancholy, he says, was produced by solitude, yet he writes—the quintessential solitary activity—to dispel it. He was a social man, and intended to publish the essays (as opposed to his journals) because he sought the human connection. And the connection survives us: one's children may read, or anyone may read, and see that something of us survives. Or if we ourselves survive, as Mairs points out, other sufferers may read, and see that survival is possible.

Writing about suffering is a special case of the storyteller's art because it produces a reaction in the readers' bodies—a visceral reaction. The readers' bodies respond in a peculiar sympathy with the writer's. It makes them wince. In this way writing about suffering tests what storytelling is able to do. The physical reaction that connects writer and reader goes beyond the ordinary storytelling situation and its reactions of tears, laughter, excitement, and so on; it thus demands the maximal authority of the suffering person. And the awakening of the reader's reaction as a physical effect affirms and revives, even as the writing itself is about the loss of the body's wholeness.

Certificates

What if I told you that your birth certificate was really a bond indenturing you to the government? Of course, you don't have your real birth certificate, but only a copy; all the originals are in a vault in Washington, D. C. At some point in the 1930s, during the height of the Depression, the U. S. Government went bankrupt. Their scheme to raise money was to *sell everyone's birth certificate* to the Federal Reserve Bank for about seven hundred dollars apiece, as a promise of future taxes. Those bonds are now worth millions of dollars each, and I can tell you how to get your bond back. But I can go further: those people born in the United States who never had their birth certificates appropriated by the government—these people are called Sovereign Citizens— are not subject to taxes by any jurisdiction, and in fact are not subject to any U. S. law. I can also, for a fee, get your certificate out of the system without a trace, and thus make you a Sovereign Citizen.

I hope that at some point in the last paragraph— perhaps at the first line—your skepticism kicked in and you recognized this for a confidence game. In fact, every statement in the paragraph is false: birth certificates were never sold as bonds, originals are not kept in Washington, the government did not go bankrupt, there is no such thing as a "Sovereign Citizen" exempt from laws and taxes, and so on. A white supremacist named Roger Elvick, a forger of bad checks, first began spreading a version of the story in the 1980s, according to the Southern Poverty Law Center, and its history may be explored on the Snopes website under "Birth Certificate" along with an interesting variety of other unfounded stories about birth certificates with which you may be familiar. Narratives setting out the scam usually at some point zero in on the fact that copies of birth certificates often appear superficially like stock certificates or bonds, and some are printed by an outfit called the American Bank Note Company.

This birth certificate scam may appeal to conspiracy theorists or to those convinced the government is out to get them, but to most of us it is obviously spurious. Yet however farfetched Elvick's scheme might seem, are we certain there isn't something of a confidence game in the very idea of the certificate itself?

We come into the world and go out of it accompanied and attested by certificates. For about a hundred years now it has been the practice in the United States to require birth and death certificates that are then filed with the county or the state in which the birth occurred, or the death.

The two certificates bookend our lives, but they have no real symmetry. The terse demand on the death certificate for "cause of death" has no corresponding question on the natal form for cause of birth. After all, the cause is always the same: a sperm in some tube or other, some confined space, encountered an egg and, wagging its tail, went in. The presence of the child, its existential undeniability, seems to be enough to warrant certification without further explanation. Death, on the other hand, can be caused by a multitude of ills internal or external: the revolt of the body, the slings and arrows of attack, or the mischances of accident. The cessation of life needs to be looked into. Like birth, it is a legal affair, but in certifying death the specifics matter. In the case of unnatural causes, this item on the form is evidence that may be used in court. Even when the body has simply worn out in use, still the cause must be specified. Sherwin Nuland writes in *How We Die* (1994) that the real cause is often just old age, but no doctor is permitted to write that as a cause of death on the certificate. "It is illegal to die of old age," writes Nuland (43). The doctor must specify an immediate cause such as sepsis or pneumonia, and often underlying causes as well.

Birth certificates are necessary now to enroll in school, to obtain a driver's license, a passport, or a marriage license, and later to apply for Social Security benefits and Medicare.

They attest to one's identity, age, and citizenship, serving as a proof of relationship to parents, showing one's place of birth and thus establishing residence of a state at the time they are issued, and thus citizenship. Their purpose for the state or country of issuance is mainly statistical and political, supplying numbers for the census, for numbers of live births. The originals of birth certificates reside for the most part in county record offices. There is no national birth registry, though states are required periodically to report birth statistics, in the past to the Census Bureau, and now to a national Office of Vital Statistics.

Sometimes birth certificates ask for birth weight, which seems a useful health statistic, but most do not. Generally, the names—and in the past, the races—of the parents are asked for, and their ages and place of residence. I remember seeing certificates that had the footprints of the newborn, and perhaps handprints as well, but they are souvenir birth certificates issued by hospitals and given to the parents, not legal documents. Those that are legal must be signed by a doctor, a midwife, a hospital official, or at the very least the parents in the case of an unattended birth.

Death certificates also have their uses for survivors of the dead. The official record of one's death is certified by a local or state agency when it has received the certificate attesting to the death and signed by a doctor or a coroner. And a spouse or heir may end up requesting a dozen or more of such certificates for insurance companies, pension funds, the Social Security system, the lawyer who handles the will, and so on. For the jurisdiction in which the death occurs the certificate provides census information, and for many decades the National Center for Health Statistics has been gathering cause-of-death information for a mortality data base.

We are much more assiduous in the gathering and certifying of such information than our ancestors were. The birth and death certificates for Shakespeare, to take a famous example, do not exist. We have parish records that tell us he was baptized on April 26, 1564, and that he was buried on April 26, 1616. We infer that he was born several days earlier—in standard Anglican practice one must be born to be baptized—and died several days earlier than the interment—polite society demanding that one must be dead before being buried. Custom has seized on the 23rd in both cases, since it not only seems a convenient interval of three days, but also happens to be the feast day of St. George, England's patron saint, so that we now have the romantic story of Shakespeare's entry and departure sanctioned by the dragon-slayer himself. The Crown had begun to admonish parishes to keep careful records of births and deaths long before Shakespeare was born, but they weren't always compliant—perhaps fearing it would make collecting taxes easier—and the officers of the Crown did not police the lapses. Anything like a central registry for births and deaths was unthought of and would have been well-nigh impossible anyway. Nor would it have occurred to anyone to give the parents a piece of paper so they could remember that they had a child on such a day.

What might we conclude about the lack of assiduity in collecting birth and death information in the past, and the near-universal practice of such certification now? The paranoid will decide that we live in an age of surveillance for its own sake. The student of history will conclude that nation-states demand documentation as a tool of enforcement. The idealist may hope that we will all somehow be made healthier by the gathering of such information. The pragmatist will say we need to keep track of how many of us there are, and what we seem to be dying of.

Are certificates ubiquitous? I offer, as evidence, the contents of my wallet. Practically everything in here can be loosely classified as a certificate. Each bill of the paper money says at the top "Federal Reserve Note," but it is in fact a certificate, signed by the Secretary of the Treasury and the Treasurer of the United States, who certify that the bill is "legal tender for all debts, public and private," that is, can be offered or tendered in good faith and compliance with law, in return for goods and services and monetary obligations. I am old enough to remember when all those bills of smaller denomination read at the top, not "Federal Reserve Note," but "Silver Certificate." Their nature as certificates was then explicit, and theoretically, they could be redeemed for silver dollar coins or raw silver bullion in one form or another. Since the middle 1960s, all denominations of notes have read "Federal Reserve Note," and no pretense is made that they represent precious metal somewhere. They are redeemable— for other notes. The guarantee that the signatures represent depends on the health and well-being of the United States government and its treasury.

A driver's license and a private pilot's license, each signed by an appropriate administrator, certify that I have at some time in the past proven myself capable of operating the vehicles specified: class "D" in one case, which I take to mean two-axle vehicles operated not for commercial purposes; "airplane single engine land" in the case of the flying license, which also specifies "private pilot," meaning I am not certified to fly people or goods for hire.

Licenses may seem to be a different species from certificates, but a look at definitions will show that one is a subspecies of the other. A *certificate* is a document testifying to the truth of a birth, a death, a marriage, the completion of a course of study, or the competence to practice a certain activity. It can also be a document certifying ownership. A *license* is a document, plate, card, tag, or badge conferring legal permission to do or own something, or constituting proof of permission granted. Certificates make up the larger category; all licenses are certificates, but not all certificates are licenses. To get away from my wallet for a moment, licenses and certificates come together in the document that certifies my marriage to my wife Katharine. The license at the top of the document, issued by a clerk of the county, empowers anyone who can officiate at a marriage to join in matrimony the two people mentioned, namely, me and Katharine. Our ages are specified, this being presumably part of our eligibility to marry. At the time, we would also have been required to be one man and one woman. The middle of the document certifies, by means of the signature of an officiant and witnesses, that the marriage has taken place, and it is headed "Marriage Certificate." A further "Certificate of Record" at the bottom indicates that the Marriage Certificate has been recorded, again by the county clerk. The whole thing is a certificate, and so are each of its components, including the license.

To get back to my wallet, there are cards there certifying that I am a member of this or that organization and entitled to its privileges. And then there are the credit cards. What exactly are these? Not certificates exactly—although they can generate certificates. When I charge something, I get a piece of paper, a receipt that lists what I've charged. The merchant gets a piece of paper with my signature at the bottom certifying that I will pay the amount indicated.

In operational terms, there is precious little in my wallet that is *not* a certificate, and I suspect mine is not unusual in the nature of its contents. If not absolutely ubiquitous, certificates are extremely common. And their prevalence leads me into some generalizations about the kind of society we live in.

The first one is that we seem to *like* certificates. There are printing companies that produce them in great variety and "personalize" them, meaning they print your name on them. But you don't have to go to a printer to get them; you can print your own. Plenty of templates can be found online, as well as programs that generate certificates. If your neighbor's dog produces puppies, you can print her up a certificate celebrating the event. Your children can each have diploma certificates when they "graduate" from preschool or day care. When I walk into the small observatory that is the home of my amateur astronomers' club, I see a wall covered with certificates—some of them mine—that commemorate members' accomplishments in observing planets, or the sun, or groups of galaxies or nebulae. A league of astronomy clubs makes these certificates available to clubs when their members complete observing programs set up by the league. I am particularly proud of the one that designates me a

"Master Observer," having completed ten of these observing programs. That piece of paper won't get me free time on an eight-meter telescope anywhere, and it wouldn't impress a professional astronomer. As the saying goes, it and two dollars will get me a cup of coffee. But I'm still proud of it. It and the reams of certificates of various sorts that are presented to people at retirement parties, Secretary or Boss's Day parties, or just Jolly Good Person celebrations, indicate we like the idea of having our accomplishments, big or small, there on a piece of paper, however much in jest it may be given.

Where does such a feeling come from, I wonder, and do we create these certificates in imitation of more solemn ones like real diplomas, or perhaps in mockery of them? Do we create them as memories for ourselves, or as cues to inspire recognition by others? In any case, we appear to like them.

And one thing we can say for sure about the certificate society is that it is a society of trust. Society works on trust to the extent that we allow pieces of paper to stand for goods, to assure us of people's competence, to represent us, and even to confirm our own identities. Once the social network grows beyond the village in which everyone knows people who were there at your birth, witnessed your marriage, saw your father buried, and so on, the necessity for certificates arises. And the prevalence of certificates means that to a great extent we believe in and trust in expertise, in the competence of men and women who do the certifying or whose skill and knowledge is certified. We believe in the guarantees—in the form of diplomas and licenses—of those who doctor us, who fly us in airplanes, who teach our children. Ultimately, the value of all the certificates that constitute our money depends on trust, and they cannot continue to have value unless the trust continues. Moreover, unless revenue comes into the system in the form of taxes, money will lose its value, either quickly or slowly. And the whole works disturbingly like a pyramid or Ponzi scheme: at any given moment there must be more money or debt notes of some kind in circulation or held by individuals, conglomerates or nations than corresponds to revenue on hand. There has to be a constant influx of revenue and even an increase as more money is printed and more debt incurred.

But trust in a huge, shifting, and—in times of recession or worse—precarious situation is something we have got used to. We even go beyond this trust to a more irrational one when we invest capitalist institutions with some notion of fair play. Thus, the exploitation of hidden bank fees, rising cable bills, or doubling drug prices does not merely anger or alarm us: it *outrages* us as being *not fair*. We expect fairness in those we have to trust in order to be and to do business in the world.

With capitalism, trust ceases to be a determiner of behavior on one side of the truster/trustee interchange. The corporate division of responsibility among stockholders dilutes it to nothing. So the certificate or contract or job description from your employer that guarantees your pension is worth a little less than a Confederate dollar. With the federal government, the largest issuer of certificates in the world, trillions in debt and still counting, the situation is less bleak to the extent that politicians who wish to be reelected are unwilling to take your Social Security away or devalue your Federal Reserve Notes.

The dark side of the trust society is the misplaced confidence in the benignity of capitalist institutions, perhaps, but trust of any sort carries with it the possibility of being betrayed. Trust itself faces two ways, is ambiguous. American innocence is matched by an equally American guile. We want to be treated fairly, but we also are willing to risk being cheated in order to get something for nothing. These dueling aspects of the certificate society get interrogated and exposed by that purveyor of bogus certificates, the con man. In literature, the confidence man is celebrated as an American type who is almost a culture hero because, though he may cheat us—that is his aim—he also reminds us just what our weaknesses are, and that we must trust each other to survive, even though it means getting cheated once in a while.

Twain, Melville, Bret Harte, O. Henry and many other American writers celebrated this hero/villain of flush times in this country, the confidence man. Melville's *The Confidence-Man: His Masquerade* (1857) is the centerpiece of this literature, a book set on April Fool's Day on a ship of fools, a Mississippi River boat. The confidence man who assumes various disguises is "a Mississippi Operator," as one character styles him. Each of his various manifestations begins by urging his marks to trust in his or her fellows, to have confidence in the essential honesty of people. Pretty much anything can be supplied by Melville's confidence man, from cough medicine and pain relievers to coal shares and even boys to help work a farm. The most effective separators of marks from their money are the share certificates of the Black Rapids Coal Company.

At the beginning of the next century, O. Henry's *The Gentle Grafter* (1908) recounts the exploits of several confidence men who have a conscience. In their world, the grafter is a gentler detacher of the sucker from his money than, say, the burglar. But even the burglar is not as bad as the Wall Street highflier. Two of Henry's grafters accidentally get caught up in a scheme to sell stock certificates in the Golconda Gold Bond and Investment Company. When they discover these shares are being bought by factory girls, old veterans, widows, and even children, they give all the money back. "Making an honest livin's better than Wall Street," says one of the gentle grafters to another as they're busy bottling up tap water colored with red dye to sell as either tonic to grow hair or a chill and fever cure. There would be testimonial certificates either way.

Bernie Madoff was no culture hero. His con was a classic Ponzi scheme where he used money coming into his fund from new marks to pay the unrealistic "interest" or "dividend" he'd promised previous fund holders. There was no investment, and thus no real interest or dividends, and of course the con could only have a limited run before it collapsed. Such schemes prey on our desire to get rich quick, to get something for nothing. In the legal con game of the lottery, certificates that fuel this desire, millions of them, litter the floors of convenience stores and are swept up and thrown away on the days the winning numbers are drawn.

Both Melville's and O. Henry's narratives make the same points about the confidence man, his mark, and trust. An honest man can be conned, because he is accustomed to trust his neighbors, most of whom deserve his trust. It is easier to con the man who has a streak of dishonesty and who wants to get something for nothing. And there is such a thing as a man who cannot be conned, but his imperviousness to being cheated is also a social barrier that cuts him off from normal intercourse with his fellows.

Certificates keep coming up in con games. Those of the Golconda Gold Bond and Investment Company are "all gilt and lettered up with flourishes and a big red seal, tied with a blue ribbon in a bowknot." I probably could not tell them from more legitimate stock and bond certificates. One hardly sees these anymore, in the age of digital banking and stock-brokering (a false dichotomy, really, since banks have been let loose from the *Glass-Steagall Act* and are the largest brokers). But stocks and bonds are the most elaborate certificates of all, having multi-colored engraved borders with crossed ribbons, curlicues, and scrolls. Baroque leaf motifs with acanthus are common. Gilt lettering and gold or silver embossed seals are not uncommon.

The ostentation is notable, especially when one compares these stock certificates with other documents such as birth and death certificates, or diplomas. These last, by contrast, are the most reserved and spare of certificates, usually without borders, simple and direct in their lettering, with signatures of school officials small and unobtrusive. It's as if the decoration and elaboration were in inverse proportion to the intrinsic value of the certificate in these two cases.

I think I'll turn on the certificate generator in my word processor and make one for myself. I'll choose the interwoven ribbon border in red and blue, my school colors. *This is to certify that* MICHAEL COHEN [I'll put that in 18 point type and bold it] *is a trusting soul, and pretty honest. He might in a weak moment go for a fund that was offering ten percent. Mostly though, he just wants things on this turning globe, in this fleeting life, to be stable.* Who will sign my certificate? By rights, all of you should sign it. But I'll just sign it myself in my role of Everyman. When I get it printed out I'll hang it on my wall between my diploma and my Master Observer certificate.

Sorry, But I Enjoy Air Travel

It's common for travelers to complain about flying, while writers and comedians make rueful comedy about it. George Carlin most notably dissected airline P. A. announcements, from the idiocy of "pre-boarding" to the jaw-droppingly naïve instruction to "breathe normally" when an emergency oxygen mask drops ominously in front of your face.

I like to travel by air. I fly my own airplane for fun, but I travel by commercial airliner. I won't try to convince you that all aspects of it are pleasant; you know better. But I have convinced myself that any unpleasantness is much magnified—or greatly improved—by attitude. Take, for example, the matter of luggage. A car encourages you to fill its trunk. Trains and buses suggest by their size that they have room for anything you can bring. Only air travel demands that you ask yourself what is necessary to pack. I realized long ago that the pilots' and flight attendants' tote on top of a small rolling case made all kinds of sense and was probably a restriction arrived at through compromise: what the crews absolutely needed for stays that could be unpredictably long *versus* the airlines' necessity to provide space for the paying rather than the paid souls on board. I may be odd in enjoying the challenge of choice or rejection of that stylin' sweater, and I positively enjoy the game of reducing weight and bulk in my shaving and medication kit.

When a jet leaves the ground, the pilot raises the nose to a steep attitude for the climb out. To a person like myself trained to fly in small non-jet planes, it's an impossible angle that I know will result in a stall, after which the plane will drop immediately several hundred feet; since we are so near the ground, we will crash. It doesn't happen, of course, because the thrust of these jet airplanes allows them to practically stand on their tails, but for me, it's one of several moments in commercial flying when I am forced to think about the imminence of death. Another such moment is the landing, which in a jet takes place at a speed entirely too close to two hundred miles an hour. Again, landing my own small plane is different: it is an exhilarating feeling of being the only one responsible for getting this puppy safely onto the ground, but it takes place at speeds that quickly slow from a hundred miles an hour to less than fifty.

I should make clear that I don't think occasionally imagining that one's death is close is a bad thing. We don't do it often enough, I believe. Those who don't fly or those fliers who are utterly indifferent to the experience never feel those moments of near-terror that others of us do: not just the volaphobes—if there is such a word—but also those of us who don't fear flying, but who carefully observe the stages of flight that are the most dangerous moments. Most automobile drivers, I suspect, have had a near-crash experience when they do momentarily feel the brush of the dark angel's wing. Flying is exhilarating for me partly because of such moments in the air, brief as they may be.

But most of the exhilaration of flying commercial is in the sheer unlikelihood of it all. That feeling when the wheels leave the ground and their unpleasant vibration gives way to smoothness and freedom, for example, is always increased for me when I'm looking from the back of a 747 across eight rows of seats and forward most of a football field's length to the front, thinking, "this is a *building* that's launching itself into air!" And even at altitude, flying comfortably along, with a drink on the tray in front of me not even vibrating a bit, I often think how truly wild and strange it is to be going five hundred miles an hour six miles up in the sky without even having my hair ruffled.

A hundred years ago Virginia Woolf noted that "Cultivated people grumble at trains, and, if they are old enough, prefer the days of the stage coach...But surely it is time that someone should sing the praises of express trains." Air travel needs its boosters, too. No excitement attends waiting in airports, going through lines for security checks, or driving to and from airports, and any one of these chores might end up taking as long as my flight. But these tedious matters enable me to experience the flight itself, a method of travel still astonishing and as different from ordinary modes of getting across land and sea as the soaring of an eagle is from the crawling of an ant. And at the end I am deposited in a different time zone, on another continent, or even half the world away.

The God Damners

Between 2004 and 2007, five books were published in the United States attacking theism and theistic religion, and all ultimately became best-sellers: Samuel Harris's *The End of Faith: Religion, Terror, and the Future of Reason* (Norton, 2004) and a follow-up book addressing that book's critics, *Letter to a Christian Nation* (Knopf, 2006); Richard Dawkins's *The God Delusion* (Bantam, 2006); Daniel C. Dennett's *Breaking the Spell: Religion as a Natural Phenomenon* (Viking/Penguin, 2006); and Christopher Hitchens's *God Is Not Great: How Religion Poisons Everything* (Twelve Books, 2007).

I read Sam Harris's *The End of Faith* in 2005 and agreed with much of his polemic against religion while being far less sanguine than he about change being possible. This book had an obvious genesis in the 2001 attack on the World Trade Center and the Pentagon, but when the other books appeared their motivation could not clearly be traced to those events. The books of Dennett, Hitchens, and Hawkins all make brief reference to 9/11, but all involved earlier research and in some cases parts or related works had been published that predated the events of 9/11. Hitchens insists in the acknowledgments section of his book that he has been writing it all his life. There was more in the air than the dust of the World Trade Center that led to these books at this time. I decided to read them to determine what they argued in common and what the unique approach of each was, as well as to explore the question: why these books and why now? The answer to the last question turned out to be a startling combination of forces beginning with the attack on the homeland but also including widespread attacks on public education and attempts to usurp political power by the forces of anti-reason.

Of course, there have been books attacking organized religion and religious belief before. As several of these authors point out, the psalmist's "The fool hath said in his heart, There is no God" should make it clear that there have always been unbelievers. But many organized religions do a good job of systematically suppressing their dissidents, and links between religion and civil governments made dissent very difficult over many centuries, so that attacks on religion did not get much traction until the Enlightenment. One of the first books to openly attack organized religion was Thomas Paine's *The Age of Reason* in 1794, a defense of deism and "natural" religion. Voltaire fired a number of satiric salvos at the proponents of various religious theories. The nineteenth century's most profound attack on biblical inerrancy and its chronology, as well as on the argument from design, came in Darwin's *The Origin of Species* in 1859, though Darwin initially did not see these consequences, and he argued in his conclusion that there was no reason to see his work as inimical to religion. All of our 2004-2007 authors have much to say about Darwin.

Bertrand Russell's "Why I Am Not a Christian" (1927) systematically dismantles the traditional proofs for the existence of God while articulating a personal stand on one organized religion. H. L. Mencken treats religions—he thinks they're "pretty much alike"—with "amiable skepticism" in *Treatise on the Gods* (1930). "The case of religion is not proved," Mencken says, somewhat mildly, but he is convinced "men simply credit to the gods whatever laws they evolve out of their own wisdom or lack of it" and that religion is an effort of the human "to penetrate the unknowable, to put down the intolerable, to refashion the universe nearer to his heart's desire."

The one twentieth-century treatment of the subject that cannot be ignored by subsequent writers is Sigmund Freud's little book published in 1927 and Englished as *The Future of an Illusion*. Freud looks at religion as one of the psychical forces that keep civilization in order, controlling its "discontents"—a topic he would explore in detail three years later in *Civilization and Its Discontents*. Religious ideas have, according to Freud, two main sources. The idea that a superior intelligence promises a new existence beyond death and underwrites the moral law is an illusion that comes out of infantile wish-fulfillment, but is still available to the grown-up, who, retaining it, can then remain a child forever. The other source he had described earlier in *Totem and Taboo* (1913): a prehistoric event resulting in the killing of the father (accidentally or as the result of an ostracized band of brothers returning for revenge) was the origin of the murder taboo as well as the deification of the father figure. About the latter event, Freud almost seems to chortle as he writes, "Hence the religious explanation is right. God was actually concerned in the origin of that prohibition." Since he equates the transformation of the primal father into God and collective guilt at the killing of the father figure with a cultural neurosis (as well as with the formation of the original sin myth), religion is "the universal obsessional neurosis of humanity." Its abandonment will be a slow process, according to Freud, and we are in the middle of it. But anticipating one of Sam Harris's thought experiments, Freud says "I think it would be a very long time before a child who was not influenced [by religious teaching] began to trouble himself about God and the things beyond this world."

*

The books by Harris, Dennett, Dawkins, and Hitchens acknowledge Freud's contribution to their subject and sometimes also mention Paine, Russell and Mencken. These books share the insistence, often strident, that we must stop considering religion as a separate category of knowing that does not have to justify its beliefs. For too long, they all argue, religion has been considered a realm apart, whose assertions and ideas were not subject to even common sense, let alone examination by reason and the methods of science. Several of these authors mention Stephen Jay Gould's formulation of this idea that religion and science are incompatible realms, "non-overlapping magisteria," each with its own questions, methods, and subjects of study. "What is it that religion studies?" Dawkins asks scornfully, and says that just because science cannot answer a question doesn't mean religion can. He calls the non-overlapping magisteria idea "appeasement" and insists that "the God hypothesis" *can* be subjected to real-world tests. Harris and Hitchens go farther. Harris says people who have beliefs with no rational justification are called *mad* or *delusional* unless the beliefs are common; then we call them *religious*: "The danger of religious faith is that it allows otherwise normal human beings to reap the fruits of madness and consider them *holy*." Hitchens lists dozens of instances where religion has acted in defiance of reasonable health practices, hygiene, and ordinary decency: getting in the way of vaccines and needed medical treatments such as transfusions, mutilating the genitals of young people, torturing children with sadistically imagined threats of eternal torment, marrying underage daughters to relatives, covering up child molestation, and banning every form of sex except one, in a species clearly designed to experiment, and constraining even that one to the right form of words and the right combination of genders. Dennett is characteristically the most gentle of these writers in his attempt throughout his book to convince believers that religion deserves study as "a natural phenomenon." For the most part, though, the gloves are off for these authors, who share the conviction that for too long believers and unbelievers alike have treated religion as if it were protected by an unbreachable barrier from real-world scrutiny.

Another common feature of these books is the dismissal, after examination, of the traditional "proofs" for the existence of God, although this examination is only implicit in Harris and is largely limited to his second book on this list, *Letter to a Christian Nation*. Dennett discusses the arguments and disposes of them briefly, for this is ground that he covered in detail in *Darwin's Dangerous Idea* (1995).

Dawkins, as is fitting for a scientist, has the most systematic treatment of traditional arguments. After offering the opinion that God's two main attributes, omniscience and omnipotence, are mutually incompatible, Dawkins settles down to Thomas Aquinas's arguments. Several of these—the unmoved mover, the uncaused cause, and most importantly, the argument from design—he says are subject to the problem of infinite regress: who designed the designer? who made the unmoved mover and the uncaused cause? Of Anselm's ontological argument that a perfect being would have to exist because existence is more perfect than nonexistence, Dawkins quotes Bertrand Russell (who merely echoes Kant) "that there is no bridge between pure thought to things." He goes further to suggest that the *only* way God can be perfect, omniscient, and omnipotent is by not existing. Dawkins applies Hume's test to the argument from testimony (what is more likely: that witnesses lied or were deceived on the one hand, or that the entire course of nature was altered on the other?). The scriptural argument has been beset by internal inconsistencies, historical gaffes, Old Testament prophecies supposedly fulfilled in order to fill in gaps, and the various agendas of the writers—all identified by scholars since the nineteenth century. As to those who point to all those admired scientists who are fervid believers, there is often a problem with defining a scientist, defining who is admired, and sometimes just counting. Pascal's Wager—that humans gamble with their lives that God does or does not exist—Dawkins says was not really suggested seriously in the first place, and in any case it's an argument for *feigning* belief rather than believing. Wouldn't an omniscient God see through that?

Hitchens takes a position that the other authors implicitly affirm, that the argument from design is the only "proof" that has ever been taken seriously. Before Darwin and Einstein, many scientists and philosophers were "default deists," writes Hitchens, accepting that the universe seemed to imply a designer, but thinkers as early as Occam knew that the argument from design was flawed by infinite regress. Hitchens gives a brief chapter to the argument, asking, "what about the faults in the design?" and using one of the creationists' examples of so-called irreducible design, the eye, to point out how it did in fact evolve in steps we can still see, and moreover, it has design flaws. Creationists often attack evolution by pointing to what they call "irreducible design"—the eye being a frequent example—and saying there is no evidence of steps along the way. And evolutionists frequently counter the design argument by asking how flawed design in organisms all over the natural world could count as evidence of an omnipotent and intelligent designer. Moreover, those religionists who think they can tuck evolution under the gown of their god and say how clever he was to have invented this mechanism, "make him out to be a tinkerer, an approximator, and a blunderer, who took eons of time to fashion a few serviceable figures and heaped up a junkyard of scrap and failure" in the process. And the other main force besides natural selection, contingency, makes no sense at all in a divine plan either: why arrange whole successfully selected groups and have them perish by mudslides in a micro-environment or asteroid collisions in a macro one?

Another common bent among our authors is speculation about when the world can be expected to get over religion. As I noted earlier, Freud thought we were in the middle of a slow process of abandoning religion. Harris thinks it might be done faster: while an end to religion may seem impossible, he says, "much of the developed world has nearly accomplished it." Dennett is not explicit on this point, but he clearly believes that evolution can alter the very conditions that in the past let religion flourish, that the need for spirituality can be satisfied in other ways, and that widespread, honest examination of religion is likely to hasten its demise. Dawkins, because he thinks religion represents a turning away from reason, believes that education is the way to address it, and not just training in reason and critical thinking, but instruction about world religions and their history. Hitchens is a wild card here. Religion, he thinks, though a feature of the infancy of mankind, will be with us "until we get over our fear of death, and of the dark." Moreover, he would not prohibit religion even if he had the power to do so, but he asks, in turn, a corresponding tolerance from religionists. Because they are incapable of providing it, since it is in the nature of religions to try to control both believers and nonbelievers, what he hopes for is a new Enlightenment that makes reason a guide for matters biological, psychological, and cosmological, and keeps religions confined.

All of these writers are in agreement that there is no God to "underwrite" the moral law that forms culture (as Freud put it). But what *is* the relation between organized religion and morality? Does religion make its followers better people? And is morality possible outside of religion? As usual the mildest answer is Dennett's: religion does good, no doubt, but something else might do as well or better. The other writers attack the questions historically. Hitchens and Dawkins examine the texts of the three major religions and can find in them only inconsistent and sometimes absurd or murderous moral maxims—and no model of moral behavior, even in the life of Jesus. Dawkins, on this last point, says the idea of atonement for original sin "is almost as morally obnoxious as Abraham setting out to barbecue Isaac...What kind of morality condemns every child, even before it is born, to inherit the sin of a remote ancestor?" As to the atonement itself, Dawkins says it is "vicious, sadomasochistic, and repellent." We don't ground our morality in holy books, say these authors. Our real conception of morality outstrips them and changes, as it has in regard to slavery, female suffrage, treatment of children, and other topics. But a rational ethics without religion is not therefore a relativist one, argues Harris. Hitchens points out that religionists impeded American slaves' emancipation and Indian independence (Gandhi's role was "weird" and equivocal), while the Hutu massacre of the Tutsi occurred in the most Christian country in Africa. None of these writers believes atheists, agnostics, or skeptics are less moral than their religious fellows. Were there any evidence that unbelievers were more peccant, Dennett notes, the religions would be onto it like a duck on a June bug. Virtuous behavior, he points out, isn't an argument for the truth of the belief, but conversely, proponents of religion must be relieved that vicious behavior doesn't negate beliefs of the perpetrator, either.

*

These authors dramatically part company when it comes to the other side of the moral question: namely, what's wrong with religion, and why do you want to get rid of it? The ways they differ will take us to the essence of each of their books.

The first of these was Sam Harris's *The End of Faith* in 2004. Harris is a neuroscientist with a philosophy B.A. and a penchant for polemic. His thesis is that all religions have basic canonical beliefs that are contrary to all lived experience, that they are all dangerous, and that moderates, by ignoring or loosely interpreting the basic beliefs, betray both faith and reason. All religions are dangerous, asserts Harris, but at the moment, Islam is the worst offender. "If a stable peace is ever to be achieved between Islam and the West, Islam must undergo a radical transformation."

He excoriates Christianity as well, from the cynical fundamentalist support of Israel (the rebuilding of Solomon's Temple will usher in the end of the world—a consummation devoutly to be wished by the believers in the inerrancy of the bible) to the waste of police resources, money, and prison space on victimless crimes, to the social agenda that will only be fulfilled when every bedroom and clinic in America is surveilled or self-surveilled. Fundamentalists and their allies want to punish what is not evil ("sodomy, marijuana use, homosexuality, the killing of blastocysts") and allow or cause real evils (choking off funds for family planning clinics, sending nonviolent drug offenders to prison, and stifling legitimate research).

Faith, even "moderate" religious faith, poses a threat to the survival of us all. "Our religions are intrinsically hostile to one another," writes Harris, and the result is violence all over the world. Moderates foster tolerance for extremism because they create a shield protecting religious belief from examination and preventing ideas such as scriptural literalism and other irrational beliefs from being publicly challenged. Those who clutch at conviction without evidence or contrary to it "belong at the margins of our society, not in our halls of power."

In *Letter to a Christian Nation* (2006), Harris addresses some of the criticisms of his previous book and continues to insist that the tolerance and hands-off attitude that moderate Christians "demand for their own religious beliefs gives shelter to extremists of all faiths."

Richard Dawkins is an evolutionary biologist, and for him the worst thing about religion is that it subverts reason and "saps the intellect." His central argument in *The God Delusion* (2006), is in a chapter titled "Why There Almost Certainly Is No God." He begins with the argument from design, which says complex things can't come about by chance, or that it takes a cleverer thing to make a thing. "Natural selection," argues Dawkins, "explains...how organized complexity can emerge from simple beginnings without any deliberate guidance." The fact that natural selection operates without an external hand does not mean that it operates by chance. But Darwin's discovery turned the argument from design on its head: while intuitively, we think that it takes a cleverer thing to make a thing, and that the pot can't make the potter, Darwin discovered a "process that does that very counterintuitive thing" and that's what makes it so revolutionary. Dawkins thinks theists who embrace evolution don't really know what they're saying, because the process that Darwin explained by which very complex things are made from very simple things without any intervention or "guiding hand," but only the mechanism of natural selection, means it is very unlikely that there is a God. So, fundamentalists who fight so strenuously against the teaching of evolution know exactly the threats it poses. One is that geologic time and the fossil record destroy the inerrancy of the bible. The second is that it takes God right out of the argument from design and substitutes a process— not chance, but a process.

A cosmological version of the argument from design asserts that it cannot be accidental that we happen to be on a planet just far enough from a star to derive energy from it but not be baked, where water can exist in liquid form and an atmosphere be retained, and so on. Dawkins reminds us that every day we discover how many more planets of more stars might come close to conditions amenable to life, and if the formation of life on any one is a billion to one shot, there would still be a billion likely places in the universe.

Even mild and moderate religion helps to provide the climate of faith in which extremism naturally flourishes, writes Dawkins, agreeing with Harris. Dawkins believes "we should all wince" when we hear a child called a Catholic child or a Muslim child or a Protestant child, and he thinks it a form of abuse "to indoctrinate tiny children in the religion of their parents."

Daniel Dennett's project in *Breaking the Spell: Religion as a Natural Phenomenon* (2006) is to break the taboo against examination of religion, and he devotes many pages to a careful answer to the question of why we would even want to examine it. Dennett is a philosopher, so his method tends toward an exhaustive question>possible answer>likely answer>objection>response>conclusion way of proceeding. He invites us to go along with him, educate ourselves in evolutionary theory, learn what evolutionists make of religion as a natural phenomenon, and ask the question cui bono? about all of its parts. We can investigate why we like sweetness, or alcohol, or what the point of sexual vs asexual reproduction is, and we can also do this with religion. Imagine we were Martians looking at humans, almost all of whom devote time and energy to religious activity such as prayer or ritual, make sacrifices such as not working on certain days, not eating certain things or anything at all at certain times, deliberately destroying valuable property in elaborate ceremonies, erecting and maintaining large buildings just for occasional gatherings. The Martians would consider this "natural" in that almost all these creatures do it, and would as naturally ask why? They might not accept literally the answer some of the humans gave them.

Dennett wants to know how spiritual belief becomes codified into religion. He traces the way folk religion is formed. What works leads to ritual repetition which in turn leads to explanatory stories. We trust to parents to keep us from danger and we trust the knowledge of ancestors, leading to the deification of ancestors. Shamans enter the picture in order to find out what the ancestors are telling us. Reflection begins to transform folk religion into organized religion and to add mysteries to the explanatory stories. Some shamans are always more adept than others at exploiting the mysteries and convincing people their cures work. Dennett asks whether religious membership works in an evolutionary way. Following Dawkins, he suggests that religious ideas or parts of religions may operate in a self-replicating way (both writers call them memes). For example, if the safety of an individual depends on his rationally choosing to join a group that espouses particular religious ideas, those ideas will be preserved and reproduce. The memes benefit and replicate, but they have to attract hosts.

Dennett does not believe true believers are nearly so common as they report themselves. Churches encourage their followers to profess and affirm belief, even though some of the followers' beliefs may be weak. So, Dennett thinks there are many more believers in belief, those who think that belief is a good thing but do not necessarily believe strongly, or perhaps at all, in God.

Dennett asks and partially answers a series of questions about the phenomenon of belief. Why should people care what others believe? Well, if your religion denies certain scientific facts that, ignored, might cause us all to die sooner, we all should be concerned. What can your religion do for you? There is some evidence that some religions improve the health and morale of their members. But the evidence is mixed, and the question remains whether any amount of health benefits could justify misrepresenting the world. Does religion give meaning to life? And, if so, do those duped by cults and con artists have meaning in their lives even though their beliefs are a fraud? Should we interfere with others' life-enhancing illusions? Even if we believe that most of the world's religions are just illusions? Dennett takes his strongest stand when he says we cannot delegate moral decisions to our priests, rabbis, and imams by saying they are beyond discussion. He agrees with Sam Harris that moderate religionists provide comfort and cover for terrorist fanatics, that it is up to Islam to reform Islam, and that all religionists must strongly condemn, by name, their fanatics and terrorists.

Religion evolved, which doesn't necessarily make it good—and Dennett never explicitly says religion is man-made, though that is implied in everything he says. More research is needed, done by people who respect both science and religion. What shall we tell the children in the meanwhile? Dennett does not go as far as Dawkins in saying that indoctrination is child abuse, but he suggests instruction about all religions in schools.

Christopher Hitchens was a journalist, essayist, and critic of culture, politics, and religion. His approach is clear in the subtitle to his *God Is Not Great: How Religion Poisons Everything* (2007). He insists that religions by their nature are incapable of tolerance, and, in "Religion Kills," he illustrates, starting with Ireland north and south, moving on to Beirut, Bombay, Belgrade and Bethlehem, all places where he has witnessed religion's intolerant, murderous nature. He mentions the Salman Rushdie fatwah and the refusal to outright condemn it by religious authorities. Even where bloodshed looks to be political or tribal, religion is "an enormous multiplier" of suspicion and hatred.

Hitchens looks at the three main holy books, all flawed by the inconsistency of their "revelations" to "unlettered and quasi-historical individuals, in regions of Middle Eastern wasteland that were long the home of idol worship and superstition." The Old Testament rules say nothing about protecting children from cruelty, nothing about rape except when they condone it, nothing about slavery or genocide except when they condone them. The whole commandments story is fantastic, contradictory, and morally repugnant. There was no flight from Egypt, no wandering in the desert, no dramatic conquest of the Promised Land, though Israeli archaeologists tried to prove otherwise. There are fine phrases, but "People attain impossible ages and yet conceive children," and God is engaged in odd arguments and negotiations, "raising afresh the whole question of divine omnipotence." The New Testament is worse. Its writers want to find warrant in the Old, resulting in the cryptic: Abraham's willingness to make a human sacrifice of his son somehow gets transmuted into God's sacrifice of his son; in the older book there is a rumor that a virgin shall conceive. The gospels are at odds about almost everything having to do with Jesus. The historical record doesn't bear out the gospels, which, like the Old Testament, demonstrate that religion is a human invention. The case for "consistency...authenticity... or inspiration has been in tatters for some time," says Hitchens. Let the religionists rely on faith alone and "admit that this is what they are doing." As for the *Koran*, it has bits and pieces of Jewish and Christian myth. It is in Arabic and relies on oral tradition heavily, and its adherents insist it can only be understood in Arabic. But its God "entrusted a nonreader (through an intermediary) with the demanding call to 'read'." This makes God look awfully provincial. "All religions take care to silence or to execute those who question them, but Islam still preaches that the infidel must die. Its book is "a set of plagiarisms" and its confusions about dates, precise language, Sunni or Shia make for a seriously unstable version of "the unalterable (and final) word of god [Hitchens never capitalizes this word]." The hadith or largely orally generated secondary literature of Islam are also bits and pieces from the Old and New Testaments, Rabbinic wisdom, and Persian, Greek, and Indian proverbs.

Theists, in a rather sad defense of their religions' crimes, sometimes resort to the argument that secular despots have killed more people. Hitchens has the most extended treatment of this defense, saying in part that modern total despots learned their techniques from religious ones, quoting Orwell that a "totalitarian state is in effect a theocracy," and writing that submission to something all-important and larger than oneself is how Mussolini described Fascism and most Christian mystics describe their faith. The Church endorsed Mussolini's Fascism initially, and the Church's anti-Semitism and anti-communism made common cause with the forces that gave rise to Hitler, to whom it essentially surrendered parish records, while ordering Catholics to abstain from political activity. Hitchens claims the Catholic Church facilitated the escape of Nazis to South America and supported extreme-right dictatorships there. The Axis included one country, Japan, with not only a religious person at its head, but an actual deity. The church in czarist Russia protected serfdom and sponsored anti-Jewish pogroms. Joseph Stalin had trained to be a priest in Georgia, tried to make science conform to dogma, as religions do, in the Lysenko catastrophe, and sought not so much to "negate religion...as...to replace it." North Korea is not an exaggeration of Communism, but "a debased yet refined form of Confucianism and ancestor worship."

Hitchens is the best stylist of the four, often funny, frequently hyperbolic, and generally more entertaining. It is he who points out, while discussing the rationalist, skeptical, and scientific-minded Benjamin Franklin's discovery of how lightning could be attracted, that every steeple and minaret now has its lightning rod. He devotes a whole chapter, "A Short Digression on the Pig," to speculation that the reason pork is taboo on the menus of several religions is that it might taste a little too much like human flesh, and thus be an unfortunate reminder of dark days of human sacrifice and cannibalism. And he asks how much human presumption and vanity is revealed in pretending that one is "the personal object of a divine plan."

*

Why did all of these books appear when they did, in the middle of the first decade of the twenty-first century? The September 11, 2001 attacks on the World Trade Center and the Pentagon provide only a partial answer to the question. Sam Harris clearly aims his first book at what he sees as the cause of these acts of terror and announces it in his subtitle, *Religion, Terror, and the Future of Reason.* But it soon becomes clear in this book, and even more so in *Letter to a Christian Nation*, that Harris has been thinking about the subject of faith in a wider context for some time. He does not believe that terrorism comes from some distortion of Islam: terrorists are only extreme in their *faith* and in their devotion to the literal word of the *Koran*, which he quotes extensively to prove his point. The book the Jews call the *Tanakh* and Christians call the Old Testament is also pretty explicit about what should happen to unbelievers and those who are so unfortunate as not to be chosen people. As all of these authors point out, if we buy into "the principle that religious faith must be respected simply because it is religious faith, in Dawkins's words, we're going to have to respect the faith of Osama bin Laden and the suicide bombers. For Hitchens, the deadly complicity of the churches became crystal clear when other religious leaders did not roundly and repeatedly condemn the murderous *fatwahs* pronounced by Islamic leaders against Salman Rushdie when he published *The Satanic Verses* and the editors of a Danish newspaper when they published a cartoon depicting Mohammed.

America was the most spectacular target of religion-inspired terrorism at the beginning of the twenty-first century. But more importantly, I believe, for Harris, Dawkins, Dennett, and Hitchens, America is the biggest battleground for the fight between religion and reason, where the territories being fought over are the hearts and minds of its populace, and where the seizing of majority political control by religious fundamentalists looks increasingly possible.

The battle over teaching real science in the form of evolutionary biology in American classrooms may seem to be the same old provincial, Snopes-trial struggle that has been going on for a century and a half, but developments in the last several decades have made it the educational issue of our time. The present form of the struggle began with the promotion of a poorly disguised religious creationism under the name of "intelligent design," in a 1989 textbook titled *Of Pandas and People*. The new disguise for creationism was necessary to try to get around a 1987 Supreme Court decision in *Edwards v. Aguillard*, forbidding the teaching of creation "science" in public schools and citing the Establishment Clause of the First Amendment in declaring such teaching religious instruction and therefore unconstitutional. The ink was scarcely dry on that decision before opponents of the teaching of evolution were working on the idea of intelligent design, which was presented to school boards without ever naming the intelligent designer as God, thus attempting to execute an end run around the Supreme Court's banning of creation "science." But proponents of teaching real science, though losing ground in the 1990s, were preparing for a showdown, which came in 2005, right in the middle of the publication of the books of Harris, Dawkins, Dennett, and Hitchens. In *Kitzmiller v. Dover Area School District*, United States District Judge John E. Jones III decided that intelligent design was not science but creationism, "and thus religious"; therefore violating the Establishment clause. The proponents of intelligent design, however, have by no means retreated after that last battle in Pennsylvania. The Discovery Institute is the main fundamentalist Christian organization in this effort, which includes lobbying efforts to convince Congress to pass so-called academic freedom laws to protect the teaching of creationism. The movement to use public funds to support charter schools which can get around the Establishment Clause is another part of the creationist pincer movement in the battle against teaching evolution and real science.

Those Christians, especially fundamentalists, who are *millenarians* believing that a huge change in the world will precede its ultimate end often believe also that the change and the end are imminent. These believers rely heavily on the Book of Revelation, the apocalyptic gospel of John the Evangelist. A prominent feature of the apocalyptic view is that before the end times the Jews will return to Palestine and reestablish Solomon's Temple. Harris believes American fundamentalists are cynically supporting Israel in order to hasten end times predictions. As Dennett points out, it's an unfortunate thing if your fellow citizens don't acknowledge scientific facts that will result in all of us dying sooner. It's even worse if they are not only praying for the end to come, but actively working for it, and one of the disturbing aspects of end-times belief includes the believers' wish to help bring it about. A nuclear holocaust, which most of the world considers a horror that must be avoided at all costs, does not represent an unimaginable catastrophe to such a believer.

During the presidency of George W. Bush it was widely suspected that he was a millenarian. No evidence was offered for the suspicion, and Bush was notoriously close-mouthed about the nature of his belief. He was a member of the United Methodist Church, the largest mainline Protestant denomination. But he also told French President Jacques Chirac in 2003 that Gog and Magog were at work in the Middle East and that biblical prophecies were unfolding there, according to *The London Independent*. Some took this, along with his offhand remark in answer to the question that he took advice from "a higher father" rather than from George H. W. Bush, as evidence that he may have considered himself the agent of God in the fulfillment of those prophecies.

Dennett's book ends by talking about the millenarians, the end-times believers, and the rapturists (those who think believers will be gathered up to heaven some time before the second coming of Christ, while the rest of us infidels will be left behind). He points out that these folks are working hard on the Internet and trying to gain positions of power, and not merely looking forward to the end, but taking political action to help bring it about sooner. He suggests a political investigation by the sitting senators and congressmen who form an influential Christian group in Washington.

Harris, Dawkins, Dennett, and Hitchens are concerned that the attack on reason by religion is a perennial concern. Yet I think there is cause to see the nearly simultaneous publication of their books in the middle of the first decade of the twenty-first century as addressing a peculiar nexus of literal attack on America's homeland, attacks on public education, and attempts to usurp political power by the forces of anti-reason.

Those threats only increased in the second decade of the century. Evangelical Christians have been encouraged by an administration they are convinced shares their values. A significant number of evangelical Christians as well as a sizeable portion of the Muslim world would be happy if the West engaged in a holy war with Islam; one widespread Muslim narrative says it has already begun. Domestically, attacks on science and on dogma-free education have redoubled. In the spring of 2018, the son of the prominent evangelical preacher the late Billy Graham called for a takeover of all school boards in America by evangelical Christians within the next four to six years. If the evangelicals are widely successful in their years-long effort to convert new immigrants and their growing families, political power that would otherwise likely be influenced by Catholicism and its comparatively progressive social program would shift to a regressive social agenda.

Do these developments mean that the wide sales of books by Harris, Hitchens, Dennett, and Dawkins have not translated into any bolstering of the causes of reason and science? If their intended audience was only the atheists, agnostics, and skeptics in the country, polls suggest that the number of such readers is slowly growing against a slowly declining religious population, but that the change could not reach significant numbers for many decades. If, however, these writers have a readership among a more substantial section—believers in belief, as Dennett would say, rather than believers in God, believers in God who have not drunk the Kool-Aid of religion, and even moderate religionists willing to entertain the idea of their complicity in extremism—then these books' readership may translate into resistance.

Trains, Ships, and Trucks

To get to Tucson's west side on some streets you must cross the railroad tracks, and should you encounter a train you can often count over a hundred cars. For me, the wait has always more interest than tedium. Rarely, the train will be Amtrak's latest avatar of the old Sunset Limited, on its way to or from Los Angeles. Less rare will be the once-common collection of flatcars, coal carriers, boxcars, tanker and cattle cars. But what I find most entertaining are the usual trains these days, composed of containers, two-deep and coming from everywhere. Often they will bear the names of American railroads: Southern Pacific or Norfolk Southern, CSX, the largest Eastern United States railroad, or BNSF, that combined the Burlington Northern with the old Atchison, Topeka and Santa Fe and is now second only to the biggest U. S. freight carrier, the Union Pacific. Ferromex, the largest Mexican railway, has many containers on trains here so close to the border, but Canada, too, has its share with Canadian Pacific or just a big CN on their sides for the Canadian National Railway.

But for me this dusty crossing turns exotic when the foreign names from farther afield come rolling over the road two at a time: Maersk and FESCO, China Shipping and Hamburg Süd, Hanjin, Hyundai and Hapag-Lloyd. Maersk strikes me as the one occurring most frequently, from the big Danish conglomerate that seems to ship everywhere. FESCO is a Russian shipping line. Shanghai is the headquarters of China Shipping. Two German companies have a lot of containers on these trains: Hapag-Lloyd, which is a merger of two large German shipping companies (I traveled overseas my first time on a Norddeutscher Lloyd freighter), and Hamburg Süd, part of a family-owned German conglomerate. And the Koreans have a couple of names that keep going by, too.

Hanjin is Korea's biggest container shipper, and Hyundai is what's left of a conglomerate that came apart in the Asian economic crunch at the end of the twentieth century. For a while as these names wheel by at a speed I calculate as about forty miles an hour, I can imagine myself in a harbor taxi cruising around the huge expanse of The Port of Los Angeles, the busiest container port in the Western Hemisphere and the place where this train was loaded not very long ago— perhaps only hours. On ships with many different flags these big boxes would be stacked six or seven deep above the main deck. The ugly ships, looking top-heavy, would have names like MAERSK LINE in letters thirty feet high on their hulls. Our little boat, dwarfed by these behemoths, would rock violently in their wakes while sea air mixed with diesel fumes.... But the crossbar is rising behind the passing train and I can now continue on my way.

The Canyon, the Collision, and the Kid Who Liked to Fly

When I was thirteen and about to enter the eighth grade in a small town outside Phoenix, two airliners collided over the Grand Canyon, 200 miles to the north. United Flight 718 was a Douglas DC-7 that had taken off from Los Angeles International an hour and a half earlier. Its 58 souls (as the number of passengers and crew are still called on flight plans and in emergencies and accidents) were on their way to Chicago. Trans World Airlines Flight 2 had also left Los Angeles within minutes of the DC-7's departure and was on its way to Kansas City with 64 passengers and 6 crew members. All told, 128 souls met in the sky on that last day of June, 1956, at about 10:30 in the morning. Flight 2 was one of the signature TWA airplanes, the Lockheed Constellation, with its dolphin-shaped fuselage and its three separate vertical stabilizers in the tail. Fuselage and tail were painted white with red stripes. I had always wanted to fly in one of those Constellations. I had constructed models of it as well as the DC-7, but the Connie was always the sexiest airplane of the four-engine prop-driven liners. I never got to fly in one; the last one was built in 1958, and all were taken out of service soon after as jets made such airplanes obsolete.

The news that night reported the crash. There was no film. Over the next days and weeks, though, there was film each night, on national news briefly and local news longer, of the crews that retrieved bodies from the crash. The main parts of the fuselages of both airplanes had come to rest on steep slopes of the canyon walls. No roads passed near the crash sites, and the retrieval effort was arduous, involving some helicopters, but mostly difficult climbing. Most of the images were either long shots showing the toilers on the slopes as tiny figures among crumpled pieces of the airplanes, or closer shots of body bags being loaded onto vans. My first time seeing body bags was shocking, and a preview of the ones we saw night after night a decade later on the evening news. The dreams provoked by those later images during the Vietnam War were not of soldiers and shooting; they were dreams of airplanes smashing into each other and into hillsides.

Because I had seen the Grand Canyon as a tourist, the TV image of its slopes, where the people and the wreckage were dwarfed by the vast landscape, was a jarring retrospective. It was an astonishing view of the Grand Canyon. When I visited the canyon, as a tourist, I had looked at it from the spots others had decided were spectacular overlooks. This time I was experiencing what Walker Percy called "the recovery of sovereignty through disaster." Percy's essay, "The Loss of the Creature," talks about the difficulty we have in directly perceiving a work of art or an object in the natural world. Instead of seeing the Grand Canyon—his main example—we look at it through our expectations of it and compare it to them. Does it look like the postcard? Are the colors as rich as those in the Arizona Highways photograph? Does it live up to Aunt Maud's description? Instead of seeing it for ourselves as "sovereign" perceivers, we have given up our sovereignty to those who have packaged the experience for us beforehand.

Percy says we'll never recover the awe and surprise of the canyon's first discoverer, but we can try various ways of seeing it for ourselves: we can get off the beaten track and see it from an angle other than the ones provided by the railed outlooks with their captive telescopes. Or we can stand behind a young child and try to experience the canyon through her surprise and delight. If we happened to be staying at the canyon when a quarantine kept other visitors away, we might be able to have the canyon to ourselves and see it as something other than a tourist magnet. Percy also imagines seeing the canyon in the midst of some great disaster, which would change our view and banish some of those prepackaged expectations. "The Loss of the Creature" was published just two years after the mid-air collision over the Grand Canyon in *Forum 2* (Fall, 1958).

I doubt that Percy remembered this particular disaster, if he was ever aware of it. But it was happening to me, now, in June of 1956. I was seeing just what it meant that the canyon sides fell away thousands of feet to the river below and were so sheer there was no place to drive a jeep or even a small spot level enough to land a helicopter. The term *rugged* gets casually applied to this awe-inspiring landscape; what it means is that the canyon is rugged or difficult for *people*. On the TV picture the small figures moved slowly, with such care that they looked impaired or disabled in some way. They were overwhelmed, trying to move and work at an unnatural angle. The camera was filming from far away, perhaps from a helicopter or the top of an adjacent slope, and when the camera operator reversed the zoomed lens, drawing us away from the scene and showing more of the canyon, the workers and the wreckage diminished almost to invisibility. These longer shots were brief, as if the TV editors feared that showing the beauty of the canyon was somehow improper, given the tragic scene barely visible on the distant slopes.

Of course, it was not only the canyon that I saw at once in an unmediated way. I saw also that my fellow humans were finally, whole or in parts, reducible to just the contents of body bags. You might be reading Plato in your cramped airplane seat, but then suddenly you could be, not a consciousness, but bone and brain matter and blood, first in the air and then on the slopes of the canyon. And when I say "my fellow humans" and "you"—of course I mean me. I'm just blood and bone and guts. I had liked to think of me as being my outside, neatly containing and, more importantly, concealing all those rude, pink organs, white sinew, white bone.

The realization I had when watching those body bags was not articulated in this way, or any way, at the time. The words I eventually put to the moment were not mine. Five years later, as a freshman in college, I read Joseph Heller's *Catch-22*, about the experience of men flying bombing missions over Germany, told mostly through the perspective of one bombardier named Yossarian. Late in that novel Yossarian reveals what he has been calling "Snowden's secret." Snowden is one of Yossarian's young crewmembers and when he is wounded, Yossarian opens his flak jacket and the boy's insides come tumbling out. The secret revealed to Yossarian was the one revealed to me by those searchers on the canyon hillsides, retrieving parts or whole bodies and filling body bags with them. The secret was that we are just this, just meat and blood and entrails. Yossarian, uncovering the shock of my moment by the shock of his, gave me words for what I had been watching during those days following the Grand Canyon collision.

I don't believe that when a writer like Percy or Heller gives us words for what we have felt, that they are somehow mediating the experience or getting between it and us. Indeed, they remove something that's between us and the experience, namely its lack of articulation. They fulfill age-old functions of art in giving expression to what we have felt but could not articulate.

I never got to fly in a Lockheed Constellation. The wonder, I suppose, is that I still wanted to after watching the results of one's colliding with a DC-7. Although I did not actually see that collision, I spent a lot of time imagining it, and I can see it still in my mind's eye. The simple message that airplanes can collide, that airplanes can crash, was brought home to me. The Federal Aviation Agency was created partly as a result of the canyon collision, and radar coverage was eventually extended over virtually all of the United States, so that now air traffic controllers can see and can separate airplanes, including all airliners and military planes, that are in contact with them. Collisions between commercial airliners are very rare in the United States now, although mid-air collisions continue to occur among military planes and among private airplanes.

My stepfather owned a private airplane at the time of the canyon crash, and later that year we flew over the Grand Canyon in a slight detour on our way from Phoenix's Sky

Harbor airport, where the plane was kept, to Las Vegas. The only trepidation I remember from that flight came from my stepfather's saying we couldn't fly into the canyon or near the rims, but had to stay high because there were often downdrafts. The necessary altitude made for even more panoramic views. This, again, was a new and spectacular way of seeing the Grand Canyon, from the ample windows of our Cessna C-175. Far inferior is the view from the tiny windows of an airliner that is usually traversing the canyon at 30,000 feet, or more than 4 miles above the height of the canyon rim.

Nor do I remember any fear when, the next year, we took our longest trip yet in the Cessna 175, flying east to overnight in Texas, spending a few days in New Orleans, overnighting again in Fort Lauderdale, and then flying the hundred fifty miles over the ocean to Nassau for a week's stay there. I liked flying in the 175, occasionally in the right, or co-pilot seat, taking the controls for short periods, under my stepdad's careful monitoring, trying to keep a straight course and maintain altitude at the same time. Even the back seat had its pleasures, especially since I didn't have to share it with anyone. But I might have known, even then, that the knowledge that airplanes can collide like that would affect me in some way eventually.

The kid who liked to fly turned into the man who likes to fly. I racked up lots of frequent flyer miles during my working life as a teacher, jetting off to conferences half a dozen or more times a year, as well as flying to reunite with family and take vacations. And then, when our boys were through college and the house paid off, I started to take flying lessons. As a private pilot, I've logged more than 1300 hours so far. My affection for flying has turned into love, but the fearlessness I had at thirteen is no longer with me. I have learned how many more things than mid-air collisions can go wrong with a flight, and I've felt the responsibility of avoiding those things when I was flying a plane myself. As a passenger in an airliner, I am free of the responsibility, but even there I feel a little fear mixed with the exhilaration at every takeoff, every landing.

Mariana Gosnell writes about the combination of "dread and desire" she feels about flying. She flew her little two-seater airplane across the country and back, including a flight over the Grand Canyon, and wrote about it in *Zero Three Bravo: Solo Across America in a Small Plane* (1993). My flying is never without a dash of fear. An airplane, like a shark, has to keep moving through its element in order to survive; I cannot pull off the road and coast to a stop to fix something that goes wrong. Danger is part of the game, and pilots speak of careful planning and best flying practices as risk management. I do not believe that most pilots like flying *because of* the risk. That may be true for some, but not for me. I like flying in spite of the risk, and endeavor to make it as small as possible.

The Lockheed Constellation first entered service as a military airplane, in January, 1943, three months before I was born. I still haven't given up hope of flying on one. There are two of them still flying, one in Switzerland and the other in Australia. Maybe I'll still get a chance to ride in a Connie, but it's probably too much to hope they'll let me sit in the right seat and take the controls for a while.

The Materialist in Her Bathtub

The materialism of Americans is axiomatic. Yet Mary McCarthy argued in a 1947 essay called "America the Beautiful" that Americans are not materialistic; what seems like materialism is actually idealism. Her argument is perhaps the least successful contrarian essay in her collection *On the Contrary*. While acknowledging that America "produces and consumes more cars, soap, and bathtubs than any other nation," she insists that "we live among these objects rather than by them" and that "the only really materialistic people" are Europeans, who still believe that money brings happiness. (Joan Didion agrees about the Europeans and says so in *Slouching Towards Bethlehem*). For McCarthy, the plenitude of America does not indicate its people's desire for plenty otherwise than as a reaction to the hunger and want of those same people and their ancestors when they immigrated here. But mainly it is frustrated desire for the fulfillment of the American promise of equality that leads to the proliferation of goods: since you can't really make all people equal, you end up giving them all an equal right to buy a bathtub. (The essay's subtitle is "The Humanist in the Bathtub"). But Americans don't want the bathtub for itself: "possessions...are not wanted for their own sakes but as tokens of an ideal state of freedom.…'Keeping up with the Joneses' is a vulgarization of Jefferson's concept, but it too is a declaration of the rights of man, and decidedly unfeasible and visionary."

McCarthy is wrong, but she provokes bathtubs full of thought about what materialism really is. To begin, her Americans' transference of aims doesn't differ from what motivates a "real" materialist. The acquisition of things cannot fulfill the materialist's dream that having them will make her happy, attractive, and finally content that she has it all. McCarthy's idealists and the materialists are both always frustrated, never achieving their ends. *Why* we want the bathtub doesn't matter as much as wanting it. Substituting a possession for something more legitimately desired is precisely what a certain kind of materialist does.

"A certain kind of materialist" suggests that there are other kinds, and this discrimination is what I will argue. Rather than try to referee a Mammon contest between Americans and Europeans, I want to divide materialists into several different bathtubs. Implied in this division is the claim that some kinds of materialism are less corrosive to the spirit than others. For most people do seem to agree that loving things is bad for you, that being too attached to possessions is bad for your soul or some other quasi-spiritual entity. You may find it more difficult to get into heaven than it is for a camel to pass through the eye of a needle, your class may be destined for sufferings such as those Oscar Wilde's Lady Bracknell calls "the worst excesses of the French Revolution," or you may experience a less drastic though no less real coarsening of your character. E. M. Forster enumerates the effects upon *his* character of owning property in the frequently-anthologized essay "My Wood." He finds himself growing avaricious, fussy, selfish, and restlessly pseudo-creative, all from acquiring a small woodlot.

I have friends a little more attached to possessions than I would like them to be. Moreover, sometimes my image in the mirror looks just like them. Are we all doomed? These thoughts, all this fricassee I scribble here, are an attempt to think about the question. Among the several kinds of materialists, I'm going to leave alone the Absolute or Philosophical Materialist, who believes not only that "We live in a material world," but that matter is all there is, that nothing transcends the "thingness" of the world. I don't think I've run into any of these. Even the big money-getters I've met *do* find a kind of transcendent value in the rush of acquisition; for them, things are nice but mainly mark their score. The act of getting is what is important, and has a sort of pseudo-athletic, highly technical, and almost spiritual value. They are in a category of materialists I'm going to look at later, whom I'll call Substitutive Materialists. The pure or absolute materialism may be of interest only to philosophers. In any case, philosophical materialism does not necessarily include taking pleasure in material things—the common description of materialism and the attitude I am exploring. Materialism as an intellectual exercise does not interest me; what do interest me are the workings of a love of stuff and its effects on the spirit.

I believe the least corrosive kind of materialism is what I call Unconscious or Normal Materialism. It gets one of its names from an often-quoted passage by the columnist Ellen Goodman: "Normal is getting dressed in clothes that you buy for work and driving through traffic in a car that you are still paying for—in order to get to the job you need to pay for the clothes and the car and the house you leave vacant all day so you can afford to live in it." Unconscious materialists are Thoreau's "mass of men" who "lead lives of quiet desperation." They do not see the lack of necessity in the routine, or, to put it another way, that necessity ought to suffice. One must be careful here, in a way that Thoreau is not careful, to separate the grindingly poor, who truly have no choices, from the rest, before one admonishes them all indiscriminately to get a grip, to simplify, and to "live simply and wisely." Goodman knows she writes for readers capable of making choices, possibly settling for less, and being happier without the clothes and the car but with more time for what they deem important. George Carlin, too, in his amazing five-minute riff on "stuff," is performing for an audience that can recognize itself in his satire. A house, says Carlin, is just "a place to keep your stuff while you go out and get more stuff." If this is not the least harmful sort of materialism to the spirit, it is at least the sort which these writers agree is the most susceptible of reform. Perhaps it's the *only* sort of materialism susceptible of reform.

More conscious of his materialism is the Nick Adams or Abercrombie & Fitch sort, the gadget guy. The gadget may be a Home Depot nail gun, a Hämmerli 208 .22 caliber target pistol, or a Lamborghini 700hp Aventador, and the gadget guy, of course, may be a gadget girl. "I take as much pleasure in contemplating the tool and enjoying its aptness for the job, the rightness of its design and the quality of its materials and construction, as I do in anything it can accomplish," said one of my oldest friends not long ago. Had he been an explorer in days gone by, his kit would have come from Abercrombie & Fitch.

Having grown up in Arizona, I still know a lot of gun owners who have this particular form of the love of guns. For them, guns are not primarily weapons that can kill, and in fact most of them have stopped hunting or never hunted at all. For them, guns are mechanisms intricately put together, machined to fine tolerances, each capable of a given accuracy to be asymptotically sought, pleasant to heft and to aim, satisfying to fire, even more satisfying to watch putting holes together within a tiny portion of a target. Perhaps I am giving myself away here. For such people, magazines such as *Guns & Ammo* print full-color, larger-than-life photos of gleaming pistols, bright and attractive as the carnations in a Brueghel still-life.

Certainly with the more elaborate and expensive machines an element of showing out is inevitable; a Lamborghini owner is not likely to be just an appreciator of a superb machine without being aware of the status it confers. But when Nick Adams lays a dry fly oh, so gently onto the Big Two-hearted River, no one else may even be around to see what sort of rod or reel he uses. When the concern with status becomes predominant in the enjoyment of things, we are no longer looking at the Nick Adams Materialist but at the substitutive sort I talk about a little farther on.

In nearly the same place is the Comfort Materialist, who takes pleasure in material things because they make her feel secure, content, and peaceful. I am not talking about the security of knowing one has money in the bank, but rather the feeling of the goods themselves...their touch and look. The cool greens and blues of old Asian ceramics, the warmth and smoothness of four-ply cashmere. Aesthetic pleasure characterizes the materialism of the comfort girl and the gadget guy both.

Substitutive Materialism is the most complicated sort because of the variety of objectives for which material things can substitute. Some, but by no means all, of these objectives are genuine creation, compensating for an early deprivation, and status. Acquiring or pointlessly modifying possessions as a substitute for creativity is the aspect of materialism that makes E.M. Forster wax sadly poetic in his essay "My Wood." "If you own things," he asks in the beginning, "what's their effect on you? What's the effect on me of my wood?" And one of the effects he explores is the pseudo-creative impulse to modify things, cut down trees, plant more trees, and put his mark on the property somehow.

> Creation, property, enjoyment form a sinister trinity in the human mind. Creation and enjoyment are both very very good, yet they are often unattainable without a material basis, and at such moments property pushes itself in as a substitute, saying, "Accept me instead—I'm good enough for all three."

The most trivial manifestation of materialism trying to scratch the creative itch is that conviction we have in the midst of a creative urge that going shopping will work instead.

Compensatory materialism—spending money indiscriminately as a way to try to fill a psychic hole created by early want or hunger, is another form of substitution. This is what McCarthy has in mind when she writes about the European traveler who "views with distaste a movie palace or a Motorola," but who is really only looking at Americans' attempt to make up for the poverty they experienced before emigrating; the European "is only looking into the terrible concavity of his continent of hunger inverted startlingly into the convex."

My mother, who'd been widowed with three children when I was less than two years old and my brother and sister were only a few years older, struggled to raise us on a nurse's salary for five years before she remarried. Later she had plenty of money, and for a while she set out to spend it as lavishly as she could, on several new houses, on Cadillacs and Lincoln Town Cars, on clothes and accessories. I think her acquisitiveness was purely a reaction against a time of terror when she wasn't sure she could keep her kids in hot dogs and Levis. But whatever its cause, her materialism went far toward the destruction of her second marriage. This variety of substitutive materialism has the same pernicious quality of other varieties because it is unquenchable; we cannot ever replace what is no longer missing or fill a hole that only exists in the past. The best we can do is turn plenty into a celebration—a feast.

The attempt to turn stuff into respect is perhaps the saddest of substitutive materialisms. Here the quality or the number of acquired things is equated in the mind of their owner with intelligence, discrimination, power, judgment, or success generally. "The primary value of possessions, for diehard materialists, is their ability to confer status and project a desired self-image," writes James A. Roberts in his book *Shiny Objects* (2011). The thing and its qualities substitute for qualities in the owner. Often a clue is the use of words applied to objects that are usually reserved for persons, such as "admire."

Last and egregiously malevolent is the form of materialism best labeled entitlement. While some who inherit money do their utmost to maintain and increase it, there are others who come by their money without effort who feel most entitled to its use. Daisy Buchanan, in *The Great Gatsby*, is one example of the sort in whom a sense of entitlement replaces gratitude. Wealth in such people, though unearned, seems to its possessors to belong to them by right.

A recent study indicates that the bad effects of entitlement may include some unpleasant character changes. In a series of experiments conducted by psychologist Paul Piff in the Berkeley laboratory of Dacher Keltner, subjects with real wealth, relative wealth, or virtual wealth (i.e., as established by the rules of a game) were more likely to steal candy intended for others, cheat at games, and lie about what they had done than other subjects with less money. Moreover, the entitled are liable to be unhappy as well as nasty. For many years now the evidence has been accumulating that—just in case you didn't believe the old sayings—"happiness is *not* positively correlated with consumption." You can find plenty of documentation in Roberts's book *Shiny Objects*.

We live in a culture that conspires to turn us into one or another of these kinds of materialists. That we should escape unscathed is almost impossible. No one would now agree with Mary McCarthy's 1947 assertion that "The virtue of American civilization is that it is unmaterialistic." Indeed, practically no one agreed at the time, though if we are to believe de Tocqueville, that generalization could have been made about America, with the possible exception of the "aristocratic" South, a hundred years before McCarthy wrote. Now America might serve as a clinic in materialism and its varieties, effects, and the study of mass media techniques to produce it. All of us in our own bathtubs, surrounded by the objects we love, are comforted by, and feel entitled to, clamoring for more.

The Maltese Falcon and The Great American Novel

In 2014 the Pennyroyal Arts Council in western Kentucky, along with many other regions and states, chose *The Maltese Falcon* for "The Big Read" they were sponsoring. The National Endowment for the Arts created "The Big Read" to encourage communities to read one book together and then to gather to discuss it at community-wide events organized around the book choice. The council asked me to be their keynote speaker for the book, and what follows is based on that presentation.

Mystery fans know that with *The Maltese Falcon*, Dashiell Hammett started an entirely new, entirely American variety of detective novel—the "hard-boiled" mystery. To be fair, Hammett has to share the credit with other writers for the pulp magazine *Black Mask*, where *The Maltese Falcon* first appeared in serial episodes starting in September, 1929. The date is significant, as I will argue below.

But the book would not have been chosen for "The Big Read" in Kentucky—and Massachusetts and Illinois and Kansas and California—if it merely offered a new kind of detective fiction. In 1998 the Modern Library put *The Maltese Falcon* on its list of the best novels of the twentieth century, suggesting that it is not just a good mystery, but a great novel. It is also distinctively American. What readers and critics have been saying for a long time now is that *The Maltese Falcon* is not just an interesting development in detective fiction; it is in fact one of the great American novels of the first half of the twentieth century.

Before we explore what makes it an American classic, consider Hammett's originality as a detective writer and the "hard-boiled" epithet. The early popularity of the book during the Depression and the movies made from it during its first ten years are connected to its appeal as a mystery and all of these things are also connected to the features that make it an enduring American classic.

The First Hard-Boiled Detective Novel

The detective before Spade was always some variation on Sherlock Holmes. You remember how Sherlock Holmes works. He shows up at the murder scene and pulls out his magnifying glass. He examines something his sidekick Dr. Watson can't even see. Then he pulls out a measuring tape and measures the distance between two marks. Watson can't see them either. Finally he straightens up and announces that the murderer was a left-handed streetcar conductor, six feet tall, with a slight limp and a bad cold, who smokes Trichinopoly cigars.

The theory behind this sort of story is that the world is readable like a book because everything leaves traces. Even thoughts leave marks; there are a couple of places in the Sherlock Holmes stories where Holmes interrupts Watson's daydreaming and tells him exactly what he's thinking. Even thoughts leave marks in the sense that when you're thinking you look at particular things, your expression changes, and so on. The world gives up its secrets to the careful observer.

The most distinctive thing about Sam Spade's world is deception. Everybody lies. Even his client lies to him. Sherlock Holmes's clients never lied. They might not have understood the meaning of what they told him, but they always told the truth. Brigid Wonderly Leblanc O'Shaughnessy, on the other hand, lies about nearly everything, lies as soon as she opens her mouth. She makes up a name, makes up a sister, makes up a story. And it is no surprise to Spade. "Oh, we didn't believe your story," he says to O'Shaughnessy, "we believed your two hundred dollars." In a deceptive world in which the client lies, the detective lies, everybody lies, even physical objects participate in the deception: the black bird is not what it has promised to be.

Spade's is also a very material world. The city of San Francisco is present physically in Hammett's pages. We could draw a map of the Stockton Street overpass area where Miles Archer is murdered from the description. And the interiors of hotel lobbies, offices and bedrooms are all described in enough detail that we can visualize them. And we learn enough detail about Spade's rolling a cigarette from Bull Durham tobacco, and later of Effie Perine's doing it for him, that it amounts to a primer on rolling your own. The physicality extends to the detective's method. Where Sherlock Holmes observes, Sam Spade bumps up against his world. Hard-boiled detective work is a contact sport. Sam Spade kisses Iva Archer, hugs Effie Perine, and sleeps with Brigid O'Shaughnessy. He is poked and pushed and eventually punched by Lieutenant Dundy, hits Joel Cairo in the face, is drugged by Casper Gutman and kicked in the head by Wilmer, the gunsel, whom Spade has already manhandled and whom he will punch later. Compared to later hard-boiled mysteries, *The Maltese Falcon* has less violence, no real fistfights, no hitting the detective over the head with a blunt object—the sort of thing you get much more of in the novels this book inspires. But there is a good deal of roughhousing and a lot of trial and error as Spade tries to figure out what is going on. He operates so much in the dark he has to keep trying to shake people up so that they'll accidentally tell him some of the truth. "My way of learning," says Spade, "is to heave a wild and unpredictable monkey-wrench into the machinery."

Spade lies, too, partly by pretending to know more than he really does. He surprises Cairo with a question from nowhere about a daughter; he throws Cairo's name at Brigid, and he generally pretends to know more than he really does about how to get hold of the falcon.

What is required to survive in Spade's world is not great powers of observation, though it turns out that he does observe a great deal. In a world of deception and violence, the detective needs a hard shell and the endurance to survive. He is alone in the world; he has no sidekick. He doesn't even have a partner after the first chapter.

The hard-boiled detective has a code that goes with the job. "When a man's partner is killed he's supposed to do something about it," he says, and he is willing to make a personal sacrifice to follow the code. At the same time, the code seems to be pretty flexible, allowing him with no strain on his conscience to take money from various people and to take advantage of everyone's greed and desire for the big money the statue seems to promise them. But the extent to which he is corruptible by money is left ambiguous. "Don't be too sure I'm as crooked as I'm supposed to be," he says, "That kind of reputation might be good business—bringing in high-priced jobs and making it easier to deal with the enemy."

Spade has a peculiar relation with the police. They certainly do not ask him to help solve their cases, as the police often ask Sherlock Holmes. Spade eats pickled pigs' feet with Tom Polhaus, and the two men have much in common. But the police are resentful of the free-and-easy methods of private detectives. They are constrained by the job. "We don't like this any more than you do, says Tom Polhaus to Spade, "but we got our work to do." And Spade is resentful in turn, because they're going to find someone to pin these murders on, and it just might be him. But he gets them to drink with him, an interesting moment that differs markedly in the book from its counterpart in the Bogart movie, made after Prohibition had been repealed. In the book, the cops aren't just drinking on the job; they are drinking Spade's contraband Bacardi. The cops are not necessarily corrupt, but Spade has no real confidence they won't take the easy way out and arrest him unless he finds them a "fall guy," as he calls it. But he isn't bothered too much by the fact that the police aren't his friends, and he says, "It's a long while since I burst out crying because policemen didn't like me."

There is more ambiguity here. Spade looks like he's willing to throw anybody at the police as a fall guy—though Wilmer is hardly an innocent. Spade looks like money is the only thing he's interested in through most of the book. But at the end the police have the people who really did the murders. Spade gives up the thousand dollars he took from Gutman as "expenses." Effie's mad at him, and he still has Iva Archer to deal with.

Another aspect of the story that differs from Sherlock Holmes tales is that the puzzle is not centered or highlighted. During most of the book we are not thinking about who killed Miles Archer. It is a dramatic moment at the end when Spade reveals that he knows who killed Miles and that he has apparently known for some time. But that is quickly lost in the drama of what he will do about it—will he play the sap for Brigid, as he puts it. During most of the story, we're not thinking about the murder mystery at all—we, like all the characters, are concentrated on the black bird.

The Great Depression and the Film Versions

A month after the first episode of *The Maltese Falcon* appeared in *Black Mask* magazine, the stock market crashed and the Depression began. By the time *The Maltese Falcon* came out in book form in 1930, the country was beginning to feel what the Depression was really going to mean for everybody. The book went through seven editions that year, and it was very popular during the next ten years, the worst years of the Depression, until the war began in 1941.

During that time three movie versions of the book were made. The first one, in 1931, with Ricardo Cortez and Bebe Daniels, eventually got shelved because it didn't meet the standards of the new Motion Picture Code developed in the early 30s. The references to Wilmer and Cairo's homosexuality presumably were not as subtle as they needed to be to escape the censors. The second movie, in 1936, was called *Satan Met a Lady*. It was a botched version of the story starring Warren William and Bette Davis, and it was so bad that Bette Davis almost broke her contract with Warner Brothers rather than make it. But it was the Depression, and even movie stars needed to pay the rent. Finally in 1941, the young screenwriter John Huston made his first movie as director, the version of *The Maltese Falcon* that most people are familiar with. Huston was smart enough to stick very closely to Hammett's actual words, and he was lucky enough to achieve almost perfect casting, with Mary Astor as Brigid O'Shaughnessy, Peter Lorre as Joel Cairo, Sydney Greenstreet as Casper Gutman in his first film, Gladys George as Iva Archer, Lee Patrick as Effie Perine, and Ward Bond as Police Detective Tom Polhaus. At five-seven, the dark-haired and fairly slight Humphrey Bogart was far from the six-foot, burly, blond Satan that Hammett describes in the first paragraphs of the book, but he inhabited the role so successfully that some of us cannot reread the book now without hearing Bogart saying the words we are reading.

In the decade before that version, though, the book resonated with Depression readers. Depression America too, was a deceptive and dangerous world, where everything looked fine one day and the next day something that happened a thousand miles away in New York could take your job away. It was a hard world physically, when jobs assumed great importance and people who had jobs were willing to do a lot just to keep them. In the story, trust is talked about often, and almost everyone breaks trust at one point or another. The country is thinking about trust a lot, and FDR makes it explicit that the economic system of the country depends on trust and people have to have it, even if it has once been betrayed. A lot of Americans changed their attitudes about the police during this time, especially those people rousted by cops because they were on the streets or because they were jumping trains to find work elsewhere or just to be on the move.

And finally there was that *dream* of striking it rich somehow, anyhow. A pipe dream, of course, of getting to easy street, of making it to The Big Rock-Candy Mountain. For most people it was a dream as futile as Casper Gutman's 17-year quest for the unimaginably valuable falcon. The black bird, is, in a line that Hammett didn't write but John Huston brilliantly added, quoting Shakespeare, "the stuff that dreams are made of." (Hammett does quote Shakespeare at least once, when Cairo is trying to console

Wilmer and Wilmer is rejecting Cairo's advances, Spade sarcastically comments, "The course of true love," a phrase from *A Midsummer Night's Dream*, where one of the lovers says he's heard that "The course of true love never did run smooth").

An American Classic

In 1999, the Library of America (a nonprofit publisher which operates with seed money from the National Endowment for the Humanities) published *The Maltese Falcon* in its Literary Classics of the United States series. Being published by The Library of America amounts to canonization; you make it and you are part of the American canon of greats. The publisher put his money where his mouth is to manufacture this book. It is one thing for the Modern Library to call *The Maltese Falcon* one of the best books of the twentieth century; it is quite another for The Library of America to put up the dough to make a fine hardback edition. "Oh, we didn't believe your list...we believed your money." What makes Hammett, in the words of Dorothy Parker, "as American as a sawed-off shotgun" and his book an American classic?

One of the reasons *The Maltese Falcon* is a classic is its style. You probably have a favorite quote from Spade's wisecracking. Mine is "It's a long while since I burst out crying because policemen didn't like me." Everyone in the book, not only Spade, has a distinctive style of speaking and can be recognized from a short quote. Think about Gutman's "By Gad, sir..." and Cairo's mincing speech, obviously being translated from his native language as he talks, and Tom Polhaus's bluff "Aw, c'mon, Sam." This command of colloquial speech is the mark of great writers like Mark Twain. There is also a sparseness to the description in the book that has been compared to Hemingway's style, and in fact Hemingway was developing his style at the same time in the twenties. But Hammett is not simply spare with words; he wants the right one and sometimes surprises you with it. Let me read a few lines of the description of Captain Jacobi of *La Paloma* as he staggers into Spade's office with a package containing the black bird:

> He stood in the doorway with his soft hat crushed between his head and the top of the door-frame: he was nearly seven feet tall. A black overcoat cut long and straight and like a sheath, buttoned from throat to knees, exaggerated his leanness....Held tight against the left side of his chest by a black-sleeved arm that ended in a yellowish claw was a brown-paper-wrapped parcel bound with thin rope—an ellipsoid somewhat larger than an American football.

The meticulous detail of this description is capped—when we arrive at the parcel that is our first encounter with the falcon statue—with the precision of the word "ellipsoid."

Hammett's plot, too, is impeccable: he keeps our minds off the murder mystery for most of the book until we see that Spade must have figured it out fairly early on. The struggle for the falcon, the promise of unmeasurable riches, occupies the center of the book, and the struggle is peopled with characters as odd and memorable as you could wish for. Hammett describes each with a few lines as he introduces them; then he lets their dialogue and their actions develop them.

But the plot is a fantasy, and the characters are mostly very strange, too. Is there any reason to make that ship's captain seven feet tall? The style helps make us believe people talk this way, even if they don't. Finally, though, I think what makes the book an American classic is the combination of features that I've already mentioned that resonate with Americans, and not just Depression-era Americans, but people today as well.

One example is the book's treatment of the police. Sam's dealing with them reflects some real things about our own relation with police. Americans have always been somewhat suspicious of the police. We know that the possibility of corruption is always present, but even without corruption there can be abuse of power. If a District Attorney or a police captain believes someone is guilty, we won't be surprised if they go right to the edge of the rules to try to convict. We as a people don't like authority. We started by rejecting the idea of anyone having a divine right to rule us. Then we built a government in which each of the three parts is supposed to watch the other two carefully and keep them honest.

Spade is an individualist without a sidekick, without a confidant, without a partner after the first chapter. He's the guy real detectives want to be, like the ones who worked alongside Hammett at the Pinkerton Detective Agency. And yet, he's not a renegade or a Rambo. He knows the system and he works it. He has a lawyer. He knows how to talk to a District Attorney. He knows what his job is.

The job in America is a moral arena. Novelists like William Dean Howells and Sinclair Lewis explored in their books the question whether success in business meant disregard for moral niceties. But the question has to be asked about jobs in general. Do you have to step on people to get to the top? Do you have to step on people to get to the end of the day? The book makes us think about the job. Of course, the bad guys have no jobs and don't want them—Cairo, Gutman, Wilmer. But others in the book do, and the laziness of the police—or their eagerness to find somebody to pin the crime on—the ambition of the District Attorney, and the desire of Spade to be good at his job—do these things mean people are inevitably going to get hurt? *The Maltese Falcon* is an entertaining way to play out some of those moral questions

At the end of the maze is the black bird itself—*The Maltese Falcon*. Of course, there's nothing American about the Knights of Malta, the Crusades, or Charles V and the Holy Roman Empire. But the promise of wealth, or certainly the hope of prosperity, is a characteristic American dream. The hope and the promise are two of the reasons people come here—the Polhauses from northern Europe, the Dundys and the O'Shaughnessys from Ireland, and so on. In this book the promise of great wealth comes from the east via the Englishman Gutman, the Knights of Malta, and the "Levantine" Cairo, somewhere from the eastern Mediterranean. The Americans, Wilmer and O'Shaughnessy and Spade himself, for a while, latch on pretty tight to the idea of fantastic wealth. The bird is the big prize, the ultimate Powerball, the lottery so rich no one seems to know its limits, though Gutman says the lower limit is two million. A 1930 dollar would have bought you fifty times what one buys now, so the bird would be worth at least a hundred million—in other words, lottery-size money. But in fact the statue is worthless.

Well, not completely worthless. While it's around, the black bird is a touchstone that shows us what each of the characters is like. Some might say that's the way money works for Americans—shows you what they're really like.

The Maltese Falcon has a very clear narrative structure; the book is very simply organized into scenes. One of the reasons Huston's movie was so successful was that he didn't alter the book's basic shape. The book already looks like a screenplay. When you compare the first two scenes of the book and the 1941 movie, you find that the first scene is a well-lighted daytime scene in Spade's office that follows Hammett's dialogue closely. The second scene begins in darkness:

> A telephone bell rang in darkness. When it had rung three times bed-springs creaked, fingers fumbled on wood, something small and hard thudded on a carpeted floor, the springs creaked again, and a man's voice said:
> "Hello....Yes, speaking....Dead?...Yes....Fifteen minutes. Thanks."

Hammett tells you exactly how to film the scene, and Huston does it. The result is a very simple, very modern-seeming way of telling the story.

Another feature that seems modern is Spade's very coldly realistic, unromantic view of his own job and life. A third of the way through the book, Spade tells O'Shaughnessy about a man he searched for in Washington and Oregon, a man named Flitcraft, who abandoned his wife and children to start a completely new life when a construction beam fell near him and he realized how quickly and arbitrarily he could have been killed. The incident, he felt, "had taken the lid off life and let him look at the works," showing him that it was not the "clean orderly sane responsible affair" he had thought but "that men died at haphazard like that, and lived only while blind chance spared them." The part Spade likes best is that when nothing further happened of this revelatory or remarkable sort, Flitcraft settled into the same middle-class suburban life he had left behind.

Spade's perspective takes in the whole picture, including the fact that life can be an affair where one dies "at haphazard like that"—especially if one goes seeking danger as a detective—but is still, even for the detective, often banal and predictable. Spade says he got it—what made Flitcraft act the way he did—but Flitcraft's wife never understood, naturally. Brigid doesn't get it either. But he's telling her that when beams and fabulous birds and beautiful liars stop dropping into his life, he's still going to be a detective. This means ultimately she's going to jail. When Effie asks him at the end how he could have done that to her, his answer is, "Your Sam's a detective."

Travels with Pat

An Evening with Vincent Price

When I was a freshman at the University of Arizona, I persuaded my roommate Pat Kent to hitchhike with me to San Diego to see my sister, who was a Navy wife. "We can stay with her a couple of days and then hitchhike back," I said. Pat was always game for an adventure. It's about a six-hour drive from Tucson to San Diego, but it took us all day. We kept getting left at crossroads, progressing in fifty-mile jumps. At one crossroads there was rain. Finally, though, as the sun was going down, we made it into downtown San Diego. I had my sister's number, so I found a pay phone and dialed it. The first hint that something might be wrong came when the operator said "Deposit $1.25 in change, please." Between us, we scrounged the five quarters and I put them in, the phone at the other end rang, and a voice unmistakably my sister's answered.

"Hi, Judy," I said. "I hitchhiked here to San Diego with a friend. We're going to freeload on you for a day or two. Where do you live?"

There was a pause of perhaps three beats before Judy answered.

"I live in San Francisco," she said in an even voice.

"What!" I said. "You've lived in San Diego for years."

"Yes, Marty," she said. "But Dennis's ship has been in San Francisco for the last year."

This conversation went on for several more minutes, but I was too stunned to listen to much of it. We were in San Diego with no place to stay and not enough money for a hotel room. We were too tired to just start hitch-hiking back—not a good prospect at night, anyway.

Our immediate solution was an all-night movie. Maybe not the best choice for some shuteye: it was Vincent Price in *The Fall of the House of Usher*. Every time I managed to doze off, there came one of those screams usually described as "blood-curdling." For me, "sleep-shattering" would have been more accurate.

In the morning, Pat remembered he had a second cousin who lived in Chula Vista, a suburb of San Diego. He managed to find the cousin's number and called. "Oh, sure," said the cousin. "Come on over. There's an empty guest house you can stay in just outside the walls of the asylum."

The asylum?

Pat's cousin, it turned out, ran a private asylum. But he gave us a meal, and I was looking forward to a good night's sleep in the guest house, which was very comfortable.

But then, in the wee hours, lights glared through the ample windows of my bedroom, and there came the sound of people shouting at each other. I looked out to see several blue-bathrobed inmates clumsily trying to climb the wall toward us, while white-clad attendants urged them to "come back down now, be calm, everything will be all right."

Pat's cousin kindly bought us bus tickets back to Tucson. I was never so glad to see my dorm room bunk.

Our Outboard Comrades

In our junior year at school, Pat and I decided to stop changing majors and change the landscape instead. We bought tickets on the North German Lloyd freighter *Breitenstein* and steamed off for Europe. It was a six-day trip on the little 8,000-ton ship, and heavy seas made the last couple of days memorable. There was a relatively sheltered bench on deck against the superstructure where the passenger accommodations were, and I sat there one night in the midst of the storm and estimated that the waves, when we were in the troughs, reached the height of the loading cranes above the deck.

Two of the eight passengers were an old ex-U-boat captain and his wife, whose company we cultivated because the captain offered us some of the very good wine he'd had stocked in the galley stores. We couldn't afford anything beyond the Beck's we drank, and we knew nothing about German wines—or any wines, for that matter. We ate with them—fish, which I remember the old man always referred to as "our outboard comrades"—and we also played bridge with them. The captain and his wife fancied themselves experts at the game. One night when Pat had had quite a few Beck's and several glasses of the captain's wine, we started a game. I bid a club, and Pat immediately responded with seven no-trumps. With much luck and little skill, he made the contract. There was a lot of squabbling between our opponents about which was at fault—they would not have welcomed my telling them it was neither—and I had some doubts about whether our Anschluss would hold. After that evening, we were not invited back for wine or bridge.

Paris and Ankara

We landed in Amsterdam after our passage. Pat and I checked into a youth hostel and then went out for drinks and dinner. On the street, we encountered a bunch of guys in a group.

"Die Passagieren!" one of them shouted. It was the *Breitenstein* crew, whom we joined for a night on the town. The pub crawl didn't end until the wee hours, when the youth hostel was long since closed. So we spent one more night on board the *Breitenstein*, this time in the berths of the crew members who were on watch.

Pat went to Paris, and I trained across the Alps to Venice, got some visas for the trip, and joined the Orient Express (in third class) to Istanbul. Pat had a friend he could stay with in Paris while he looked for work, while I was headed for Ankara, where my brother, stationed there in the army, had quarters large enough to put me up. In the spring, I started back through Greece and Italy, and eventually to France. Pat was working for SHAPE. I was ready to head back to the States.

April in Paris, with Dwarves

In April of 1964, Pat and I witnessed a fistfight between two men, both dwarves, outside a bar on the Boulevard de la Motte-Picquet in Paris. It did not occur to me until much later that dwarf-tossing might have been involved.

I spent the whole month of April, including my twenty-first birthday late in the month, in Paris that year. Everything about that time was memorable and extraordinary, but nothing more strange than the dwarves' fistfight. Pat and I were usually out in the evenings, bar-hopping, finding a good cheap restaurant in the student quarter, or just enjoying the passing scene. That night, we were walking past a bar near where he lived in the 7th arrondissement, when two dwarves tumbled out of the door, got up, and proceeded to slug each other. After the surprise, my reaction—and I think it was shared by a number of those around me—was what do we do? I wouldn't have felt any hesitation stepping, with some help, into a fight between ordinary-sized people if I thought it needed stopping. Fights that are unequal, or in places where others might get hurt, often have people separating the combatants. But we were all strangely frozen as spectators. Would these two appreciate such a gesture from big people? It struck me as a delicate question. Of course, some of the big people were enjoying it. After a short, fierce engagement, the two men stopped fighting; one went back in the bar and the other down the boulevard.

I'd almost forgotten this incident until one day, listening to an economist talking about strange economic arrangements that some people want to ban even though they might benefit the participants, I heard him mention, in passing, dwarf-tossing as an amusement in bars. Of course, I had to look that one up. Apparently one of the places dwarf-tossing used to be popular was Paris. (It was banned in Florida in 1989 and in New York a year later.) Though a community in the Paris suburbs banned dwarf-tossing, and had its ban upheld by an appeals court in 2002, dwarf-tossing is probably still legal in metropolitan Paris.

Did the fisticuffs on la Motte-Picquet have something to do with dwarf-tossing? One of the additional strange things about the fighting dwarves is that they were dressed up—they were wearing suits and ties. The bar from which they had emerged did not look at all an up-tone place (how I wish now I had gone in to look around), and it occurs to me they might have been dressed for an act, or, perhaps, dressed to go out somewhere after taking off other costumes; dwarf-tossing sometimes involves padded costumes or, more bizarrely these days, Velcro-clad dwarves who are thrown at Velcro-covered walls. And since I'm so wildly speculating, were they fighting about the act? Turf, technique, or the esthetics of the thing? I'll never be able to find out what was behind that little people's mêlée in that memorable Paris spring.

The Last Excursion

In the summer of 1988, four years before Pat died of colon cancer, I was in Washington for a fellowship and, since he lived nearby in Virginia, we got together often. One scorching July day—I remember it as 104 degrees, and certainly all morning I had heard the sirens of ambulances picking up collapsed sightseers at tourist spots—Pat picked me up at my place in Foggy Bottom and we headed for Mount Vernon, which I had never visited. Despite their pleasant setting on a hill overlooking the Potomac, the house and outbuildings were radiating the July heat. The little rooms, the low ceilings, and the few windows to provide ventilation shocked me. I couldn't help thinking about the constant stream of visitors in the house to see the Great Man, the dinners with formal attire: the men in waistcoats, frock coats and stocks stifling their throats; the women in full length, long-sleeved dresses and petticoats. How did they do it? I must have asked the question aloud, because Pat said it wasn't as bad as Ajo in the summertime. The little Arizona copper-mining town where he grew up did get prodigiously hot in July.

Full Stop

Sitting on the terrace of the Monterey Court on a recent mild February evening in Tucson, listening to my neighbor John Coinman finish a song ("Forty Crosses on the Road to Ajo") about the loss of his old friend, my attention turned inward. When you lose a friend who was the companion of your youth, your blood brother with whom you shared all the hope and determination of conquering the world with your art—when this happens to you and you are my neighbor John, you sing a song about it.

My friendship with Pat Kent, dead these twenty-five years now, was like John's with his friend: hitchhiking together through the Southwest, dropping out of college together, getting as far from home as we could, dreaming of being writers. What happens when you lose a friend so close you finish each other's sentences? You finish your own sentences, I guess.

It's an old, old story, older even than the Greek epics. Gilgamesh's friendship with Enkidu, the tamed wild man of the forest, begins with a fight that ends in their sworn fellowship. Together they kill the Bull of Heaven sent by the vengeful goddess Ishtar. Together they tackle the most fearsome creature imaginable, the Humbaba. Gilgamesh strikes the first blow, Enkidu the second. We are not told who strikes the third blow that fells the monster; thus does the poet indicate the closeness of their cooperation. To find the creature, Gilgamesh and Enkidu have braved the fearsome wood that stretches ten thousand leagues in every direction. But Enkidu has a dream: The gods have decided that one of them must die. Enkidu knows that Gilgamesh is the hero of this poem, so it is Enkidu who sickens and dies. The author of the Gilgamesh epic, writing at the end of the third millennium before Christ, knows the varied feelings the death of a friend engenders and how these are mixed.

When my friend Pat died, he and I were in our late forties. The bloom of youth was off, but there was plenty of world left to conquer. Pat had increased the number of languages for which he did technical translations to twenty-two—he was a remarkable linguist. I had published my fourth book and was a couple of years from being named chair of my college department. His cancer had already metastasized when he was diagnosed, and it took only about a year to kill him. This death brought me stinging grief followed by the emptiness of loss. But other feelings forced themselves into the grief. The bloom of youth was off for sure with the realization of my own mortality. Pat's death was the closest that had yet touched me. A kind of futility replaced my anticipation of the future.

Montaigne's great friend Étienne de La Boétie was only thirty-two when he died, and Montaigne was thirty. He celebrates their comradeship in one of his first essays, "On Friendship." Astute readers, including Virginia Woolf and Montaigne's translator Donald Frame, have written about his need to write to preserve his mental health, as well as the fact that the first series of essays was written in the half dozen years after the death of his friend. He tells us himself that his first idea about the form his writing should take came from letters written to La Boétie. But he happily settled on that form which, if he didn't invent it, certainly traces its modern origin to him. For the *New Yorker* writer Adam Gopnik, the form of the essay itself reproduces the wish to communicate in this personal fashion: It says to the reader, "You're my best friend."

Gilgamesh experiences a profound fear of his own death following that of his friend. He goes on a quest for eternal life. After a number of adventures, the futility of the quest finally gets through to him, and he returns to the city of Uruk, whose walls he built himself, and, in the words of one of his translators, Nancy Sandars, he "engraved on a stone the whole story."

Grief, thoughts of one's own mortality, and a stab at immortality for ourselves, our dead friends, and our friendship: Sing the song, build the city, preserve the story in stone, write the essay.

Plato's Handbook

A mericans love the potential of a complete education compressed into a big book box: for example, the Harvard Five-foot Bookshelf; the Great Books; or various encyclopediae including *Britannica* itself after its acquisition by the University of Chicago. Americans also have a genius for packing lots in small spaces: for example, a First Aid Kit in a sardine can, *The Earthquake and Zombie Apocalypse Survival Kit* in a Backpack, and the silicon chip. Together these qualities give rise to one of the country's distinctive products: the omnium-gatherum handbook. Because the everything-about-your-subject-in-a-book-that-fits-into-your-pocket is strictly an impossibility, it may be useful to get a first sense of the handbook concept by looking at a fantasy version. I suspect most people of a certain age who were kids in America will remember *The Junior Woodchucks' Guidebook*.

I recall one frame of a Donald Duck comic in which his nephews Hughie, Dewey, and Louie are in the woods where there may be wild Indians. They come upon a little assembly in the crotch of a tree consisting of an arrow (my memory failed me here; it was a spear) pointing at an egg. They are puzzled until one of them pulls out his *Junior Woodchucks' Guidebook* and announces that this sign means, "Go back where you came from" (Walt Disney's *Uncle Scrooge #18*). The Woodchuck Guide had an answer for every possible outdoor question in the pages of one little volume. Carl Barks invented the Junior Woodchucks in 1951 (Walt Disney's *Comics and Stories #125*) and the guidebook in 1954 (Walt Disney's *Uncle Scrooge #5*). The *Junior Woodchucks' Book of Knowledge* later became, briefly, The *Junior Woodchucks' Guidebook and Reservoir of Inexhaustible Knowledge* (Walt Disney's *Uncle Scrooge #12*) before dropping the extravagant claim of that last part, but it remained a wonder. It was small enough to fit into one of the little nephews' backpacks, yet it contained not only the answer to every woodlore question, but in later episodes all kinds of esoteric information about the labyrinth of King Minos on Crete, how to deal with dragons, and everything your duck family will ever need to know about the lost city of Atlantis. It may have been suggested somewhere in the comics that the *JWG* was a multi-volume book, but that doesn't make it any more believable. And of course, if it was in many volumes, it's still a marvel that a nephew always managed to have just the right volume for the task at hand in his backpack.

In its literally fantastic inclusiveness, the *Junior Woodchucks' Guidebook* poked fun at the *Boy Scout Handbook*—or perhaps not at the book itself but at the innocent conviction of scouts that their handbook really did contain all useful information. The *Boy Scout Handbook* encountered the problem of all real handbooks in its first edition of 1911 and every subsequent one. No real book can be a reservoir of inexhaustible knowledge, and handbooks are further limited by being intended as field guides; portability is always an issue.

Ernest Thompson Seton wrote a handbook for the new organization of the Boy Scouts of America in 1910, but it was superseded by *Boy Scouts of America: The Official Handbook for Boys* in 1911. And, since we are looking at official matters, it didn't get the actual title of the *Boy Scout Handbook* until the sixth edition in 1956, which had a cover painted by Norman Rockwell. I will talk about the *Boy Scout Handbook* as if it had that title from the beginning.

In the 1911 edition, Seton wrote two sections; the one on "Woodcraft" shows you how to recover when you get lost, how to measure the height of trees and the distance across a river, but also how to build a log cabin. "Health and Endurance" advises the scout to avoid coffee, tea, alcohol, and tobacco. Exercise, proper diet, and hygiene are the way to stay healthy, and a convenient eye chart is included so the scout can check his own eyesight. Chivalry is a main topic, as are kindness, self-sacrifice and unselfishness, fair play, loyalty, and courage. The admonition to do a good deed each day is illustrated with pictures of a scout protecting a child from a mad dog and of another scout helping an old lady across the street. Religion, too, is stressed, "No matter what the boy may be—Catholic, or Protestant, or Jew." "Work, Not Luck" is one heading. The directions for tying a square knot appear on page 21, and there is an Appendix with 8 pages of equipment you can order.

Scout protecting child from mad dog

Paul Fussell wrote an appreciative essay in response to the 1979 edition of the *Boy Scout Handbook*. Fussell decides he likes some of the handbook's advice. "There's more emphasis now on fun and less on duty; or rather, duty is validated because, properly viewed, it is a pleasure." A little bit too much "free world" and Deism, thinks Fussell, but the latter is "so broad it's harmless." The politics, are, if anything, of the "slightly archaic liberal" variety, and the advice generally sensible: putting the campfires "cold out," and "looking objectively outward and losing consciousness of self in the work to be done."

The modern handbook has grown to nearly 500 pages. Its current manifestation is the 12th edition, which commemorates the American Boy Scouts' centennial. The book is much like the 9th edition Fussell examined, and still celebrates leadership, citizenship, and fitness, while offering practical advice on camping, navigation, and nature in general, with an emphasis on leaving no traces when we have been out there (this edition is printed on recycled paper). But even at 500 pages, the handbook acknowledges its inadequacy for the task of providing comprehensive scouting know-how. From the very beginning the handbook has deferred to auxiliary sources such as pamphlets and other handbooks for the fulfillment of requirements for its merit badges—more than a hundred certificates of accomplishment in individual areas of expertise such as camping, lifesaving, cooking, first aid, and more community-spirited ones such as citizenship and public health. Some of the original 57 badges have been discontinued (carpentry, pathfinding, signaling, and stalking—now called tracking—were reinstated in 2010) while others are thoroughly up-to-date and involve the use of GPS and other modern wonders.

*

Handbooks are reference works that are intended to be carried around. What comes to mind when you think of a such a guide may depend on your work, hobbies, or home projects. My old friend who went from being a Navy spook in the Cold War to renovating houses thinks right away of the *Pocket Ref*, a reference book of science, engineering, construction, auto repair, and other endeavors, with tables, conversion formulae, and information about math, money, metals, maps, and more, all fitting in your shirt pocket. He used other handbooks, I'm sure, when he was chasing Russian subs and cracking their codes.

Handbooks accomplish a relatively small group of purposes. Some handbooks are *constitutive*: the trifold that instructs you how to assemble your Ikea chair, for example, or the United States Constitution. They tell you how to put it together or how it's put together. The constitutive function has always been there in the *Boy Scout Handbook*, from the time Ernest Thompson Seton told the scouts how to put up a tent in the 1911 handbook until the latest editions; for example, in the twelfth edition (2009) a pamphlet pasted inside the front cover instructs *How to Protect Your Child from Child Abuse: A Parent's Guide*; the pamphlet is also available in Spanish.

A lab manual is one form of handbook which goes beyond the constitutive to a further function of inviting, if not contemplation, at least reflection. For example, the manual instructs you how to separate water into its component parts of hydrogen and oxygen by placing the ends of two wires from a battery into water and inverting full test tubes, partially submerged, over each. It tells you to observe the bubbles rising into the tubes, noting that one of the tubes, that over the positive wire of the battery, is filling with gas twice as fast as the other. When that one is full, the directions say to cover its mouth with your thumb, lift it from the water, and bring a lighted match to its mouth as you uncover it. Then enjoy the satisfying pop! Follow the same procedure with the other test tube, but this time insert the match into the tube. No pop this time, but the match glows brighter.

These steps are only preliminary to the one that may be less clearly spelled out in the manual but is in fact the whole point of the exercise: your standing back and thinking about what just happened. This step, which we might call the *Socratic* function of the lab handbook, often requires that you think about realities and connections that are not strictly visible, but require inference. Thus you have separated the liquid water into two gases, one flammable and the other a flame accelerant. There were two parts of the former gas to one of the latter. Even if you had no name for the hydrogen and the oxygen thus separated, you would nevertheless have arrived at a startling revelation about the nature of liquid water and could write its formula even without names as X2Y.

It is worth thinking about the origin of handbooks, which began as contemplative and spiritual rather than aimed at material objects; the *vade mecum* ("go with me") was most often a religious, meditative manual such as the *Spiritual Exercises* of Ignatius of Loyola. The much earlier *Enchiridion* or handbook of Epictetus was a series of admonitions intended to preserve the reader's evenness of mind and temper, written by a Stoic philosopher.

*

In my house, the handbook most in use is a birding field guide, and such guides are good places to look for the problems their makers face in both inclusiveness and in that last but perhaps most important function: the assimilation and contemplation of what we have learned. Guides before Roger Tory Peterson's breakthrough in bird identification were mostly lists, clumsily illustrated, if pictures were provided at all. Peterson's *A Field Guide to the Birds* (1934) took a brilliantly obvious idea from Ernest Thompson Seton—not from the scout handbook but from *Two Little Savages* (1903): a crude drawing of ducks in profile in that book showed their distinctive shapes and something of their different markings. Peterson begins his guide with endpapers showing birds drawn to scale in black silhouette, thus driving home the idea that they can be identified, even in poor light and at a distance, by their sizes and unique shapes, along with their customary postures. He goes on to illustrate, in many black-and-white and colored drawings, the birds that are described in his guide, in short paragraphs of 10-20 lines. Other drawings concentrate on the tails of Jaegers, bills of Plovers, and postures of ducks on land (in silhouette again). Short lines on the complete drawings point to features— field marks—that are listed on an opposite page. The point, Peterson says in the preface, is a method "so that any bird could be readily and surely told from all the others at a glance or a distance." Birdwatching has already become birding on Peterson's first page, and what exactly is birding? It is a game in which the object is "to list as many birds as we can in a day." To that end, a checklist follows the preface in the second edition. I am being unfair to Peterson in taking some of his words out of context. But with the beginning of the modern bird guide—and Peterson's book deserves this distinction—a tension is set up between getting that bird identified versus something more. That something more is why we are looking at birds in the first place.

Peterson was not my beginning field guide, but rather the first edition of the *Golden Guide, Birds of North America*, which had come out in 1966, the year before I married and began watching birds with my wife Katharine. This paperback made clear right from the spectacular cover image one of the reasons we look at birds: three buntings are illustrated in full color: the soft blue and chestnut Lazuli Bunting, the intensely-hued Indigo Bunting, and the most colorful of North American birds, the blue, red, and green Painted Bunting.

While the early Petersons were not available in paperback, the *Golden Guide* was at once the smallest, most pocket-pliable, and the cheapest of the guides. In many respects the *Golden Guide* was cheap in production as well as price: its range guides were tiny and nearly indecipherable. It also wasted precious space on its essentially worthless "sonograms," which were attempts to picture birdsong by plotting pitch against time in a diagram. But the illustrations by Arthur Singer somehow transcended their printing economies and became the images against which I read the more imperfect world of birds in the wild. I carried my copy of the 1966 *Golden Guide* until the pictures on the cover were scarcely recognizable. By that time the *National Geographic's Field Guide to the Birds of North America* had become, in its own marketing phrase, "the birders' bible."

The National Geographic field guide changed the game again half a century after Peterson. Nearly a thousand birds were illustrated in every significant plumage, some in flight and others in typical attitudes. More than twenty artists worked on the book, and dozens of experts contributed to the descriptions. The book was organized according to the latest classifications of the American Ornithological Union, so in the course of becoming familiar with the families of birds in the guide's plan, one may form something of their "presumed natural and evolutionary relationships," as well as finding that their order conformed to the latest A. O. U. checklists. Range maps were clear and sometimes zoomed in on an area of as few as three states. *The Geographic Guide* worked hard to describe songs and call notes. Overall appearance of birds and significant field marks in the descriptions were minute and technical enough to necessitate six pages of introductory text and labeled drawings of heads, wings, tails, and variations in molts and plumage; anyone reading the introduction will learn a great deal about birds before even trying to identify one. This instructive material was a huge expansion of similar half-page illustrations of parts of a bird found in previous bird books. And there are frequent acknowledgments in the text that, for example, the distinctive flicking of tails of flycatchers is behavior "not only useful for identification but fascinating to watch."

And then, just when everyone thought the era of the single author-and-illustrator field guide was at an end, David Sibley came out with his own guide in 2000. *The Geographic* had already gone through four editions at that point. Sibley not only provides illustrations of sexual dimorphism, juvenile and yearly phases, and fall versus breeding plumage, but he also illustrates nearly every bird in flight, from above and below. Moreover, *Sibley* can sometimes be more helpful than *The Geographic* on behavior. I know that my wife and I are not the only birdwatchers to have found the necessity of having both guides on hand to settle a question of identification. "It is no easy matter, this trying to get to know the birds, says the 1911 edition of the *Boy Scout Handbook*.

The Geographic quickly became standard equipment for beginning as well as experienced birdwatchers. But it was an uncomfortable *vade mecum*: it wouldn't fit into the hip pocket of my jeans, so I had to stow it in a backpack, where it couldn't be consulted quickly. And despite the *Sibley*'s size— over nine by six inches—a lot of my friends switched to it, though it was a book they checked when they got back to the car rather than one they tried to slip into their pockets. These two guides together weigh almost five pounds and each has around five hundred pages. Thus, the closer we get to an ideal of inclusiveness in handbooks, combined with an approach fostering genuine learning, the farther we get from a little book even a duckling could carry and the closer we get to a five-foot bookshelf of reference volumes.

Though I find the size of these new guides a little inconvenient, I have to admit that these books have come a long way from the nearly exclusive purpose of identification toward an ideal of birding books—guiding you through the whole of the subject. *The Geographic* and the *Sibley*, if you read carefully and thoroughly, will teach you about bird morphology, behavior, habitat, and migration.

*

HANDBOOK OF

NATURE-STUDY

For Teachers and Parents

Based on the Cornell Nature-Study Leaflets, with Much
Additional Material and Many New Illustrations

By ANNA BOTSFORD COMSTOCK, B. S.

Assistant Professor in Nature-Study in Cornell University; Author of How to Keep Bees,
and Ways of the Six-Footed; Illustrator and Engraver for Manual for the
Study of Insects and for Insect Life

EIGHTH EDITION

ITHACA, N. Y.
THE COMSTOCK PUBLISHING COMPANY
1918

I'm always searching for an ideal, a Platonic handbook, I
must now stop stalling and try to describe it. Since it's an ideal,
examples only approach it. If a handbook as sophisticated
as *The Geographic* and the *Sibley* existed for snakes, another
for mammals, yet another for geology, another for trees and
shrubs, and still another for wildflowers, I could at least pile
them all in my backpack and totter off—but wait, there has
to be another for weather, and yet another for the night
sky. And ideally, they would be all together in one handy—
literally one-handable—form, like *The Junior Woodchucks'
Guidebook*.

Clearly that is not going to happen. But I think an ideal approach has been taken in two handbooks I've come across. One is a nature guide as old as the *Boy Scout Handbook* itself, and the other is comparatively new.

Anna Botsford Comstock's *Handbook of Nature Study* has been in print continuously for over a hundred years, through many editions but few real changes. Comstock is still a great resource for homeschooling; the seventh edition of 1918 is available for download free, and the 34th edition can be bought in paperback. Beginning with the familiar, her handbook starts with backyard birds. She has students looking at feathers for form and for function as clothing, ornament, and machine for flight. After looking at eyes, ears, beaks, and feet, she goes on to birdsong, attracting birds, their practical value, and their migration.

With birds and then other animals, Comstock starts close by and gradually moves outward to field and stream, progressing from the familiar to the less familiar, always with the emphasis on discovery and detail. She tries to get the student to attend to how an animal feeds, its habitat, its nest or burrow, and the way it fits in with its immediate environment. She moves on to plants, fungi and molds, streams, weather, and the sky. She covers familiar territory, and doesn't get beyond the end of the woods, but she encourages a close look at detail as well as a view of the big picture. Comstock's is a somewhat specialized handbook, intended for nature study by students and their teachers. Its method is Socratic, not in the sense of dialectic questioning, but in the epistemological implications of Socrates's method: the seeker after knowledge cannot achieve it by being told answers, but must find her way to knowledge by her own efforts. Her project is not merely giving the denizens of nature names and providing categories into which they can be put; she aims for nothing less than making nature genuinely and thoroughly familiar. These are our own ponds and woods; shouldn't we know them intimately? Such an approach has enabled the Comstock handbook to survive despite its small and dark photographs, its heft and size at around 900 pages, and its language, that often strikes the ear as quaint and dated.

Another handbook that approaches my Platonic ideal is one my wife and I consult often at our house in the Tucson Mountains. Roseann and Jonathan Hanson's *Southern Arizona Nature Almanac* (2003). The authors quote Ernest Thompson Seton that a nature book must have more than facts—it must have personality, and the Hansons' book rises to the challenge. They point out that we don't have a chance of identifying, let alone learning anything about a bird or a wildflower unless we have a contextual guide, which is what they set out to give us. The subtitle identifies the guide's purview as Pima County and all of southern Arizona below the 30th parallel from Tucson west to the California border. The authors wisely have not tackled the equally rich Whetstone, Huachuca, and Chiricahua mountains along with the San Pedro and Sulphur Springs Valley to the east.

The *Almanac* zeroes in on the wildlife—and to a limited extent the geology—of low and high desert floor, the pine-oak woodlands and mixed coniferous forest of the "sky islands" of the Santa Catalina, Rincon, and Santa Rita Mountains, and riparian woodland along perennial streams and rivers at both low and high altitudes, and does so for each month of the year. So we're already being educated about what to expect just by locating ourselves in space and time on any given workday or weekend outing. This specificity makes identification a process of recognizing a juniper, a brittlebush, a Lark Sparrow or a Coatimundi within its environment, which leads seamlessly to what blooms when, what these creatures eat, and when we're likely to be rained on during the year's two rainy seasons.

The Hansons also think we ought to know what to see in the night sky each month and what temperatures to expect; their weather data comes from the low desert at Yuma, Tucson's airport at 2,500 feet, and a station near the summit of the Santa Catalina Mountains. Within its limitations the *Almanac* comes very close to my Platonic ideal.

But the limitations of the *Almanac* are great. It has to be supplemented with a backpack full of other guides, and indeed the authors not only recommend other guides, but they talk about stocking their backpacks with them when they hike in the Santa Catalina Mountains or the Tucsons. Moreover, the Almanac is specific to the mountains and valleys that make up the northern Sonoran Desert in southern Arizona.

*

The *Junior Woodchucks' Guidebook* was misnamed from its beginnings. Had it been merely an imaginary rival to the *Boy Scout Handbook*, it should have been called a *handbook*; *guidebook* or *guide book* has always been the term for a travel guide—a book intended to replace a human guide to a tourist destination. But the *JWG* always aspired to more than handbook status—it wanted to be the reservoir of inexhaustible knowledge. Now that we have in Wikipedia an electronic, universally accessible *Junior Woodchucks' Guidebook*, we can see that the *JWG* really wanted to be a virtual encyclopedia, before such a thing had even been thought of. With its realization as the online free-access source that aspires to put together the sum of all human knowledge, comes clarification of why the *JWG* would never really have competed in the arena of my Platonic handbook. My handbook goes beyond giving answers and concerns itself with *finding* answers. Socrates knew he couldn't impart knowledge by lecturing to his followers because his view of knowledge was that it had to be acquired by the knower in a dialectic process. Aside from the fact that the sum of all human knowledge includes techniques that can't be learned from a book's or page's directions, even the mere answers we look up in *Wikipedia* do not impart knowledge in the Socratic sense. Even a parrot can repeat an answer. You can download all of *Wikipedia*; it's only about 50 gigabytes now. But the ultimate handbook is as large as the world.

Learning Ancient Greek at the Downtown Y

A couple of years ago my old friend Hugh Lawson decided to go back and try to learn to read Latin—he and I both had two years of it in high school, and though odd bits of it seem to have stuck in both our cases, mostly vocabulary, he admits to having forgotten most of his high school Latin. He now spends an hour or two a day reading Latin authors in their original tongue. Of course he gets questions from many of his friends. "What's to like about a dead language like Latin?" they ask him. "I'm not sure I *like* it," is his reply, "I like having figured out what a Latin sentence means."

This answer speaks to my own interest in Greek, which Hugh's example inspired me to finally tackle. "Why would I try to learn Greek?" I ask myself. And the simple reply is, "I would like to be able to read Homer, to get familiar with the Odyssey, especially, in its original language rather than in the oddly very different translations I have read over the years, beginning with E. V. Rieu's Penguin edition—the very first Penguin Classic, by the way—that we read in my sophomore Humanities class in college, to the Richmond Lattimore version that was hailed as the first truly poetic translation since Pope, to the Robert Fagles translation I used in the Humanities honors class that I taught for years."

So, the effort here is learning not just ancient Greek, but Homeric Greek. Does this seem a little specialized, not to say chimeric? I wanted to read Homer. As I discovered when I got into it, Greek changed remarkably little over the millennium from Homer to the writing of the New Testament, and a student learning Homer's Greek can, with a dictionary for the quite different vocabulary, read Greek from the classical period of the great dramatists. A few grammatical and usage adjustments equip the learner for New Testament Greek.

But all this is beside the point. I wanted to learn Homer's Greek, and I would have gone for it even if he was the only one I could read with it. If this strikes you as odd, I can only invite you to consider a converse situation with someone eager to learn English for a particular reason. I am deeply fond of Shakespeare, read him often and watch performances when I can. My reading of Shakespeare, with fair ease and much pleasure, by no means came from merely being a speaker of English. I trained to read Shakespeare by studying my language and its history as well as by reading many other authors. Suppose for a minute that I were not an English speaker but a speaker of, say, modern Greek. Suppose also that I had read Shakespeare in translation, loved him, realized his greatness, and had a hankering to read him in the original. Would it be a mad scheme to try to learn to read him in "Shakespearean" English? The difficulties would be great. There is that pesky alphabet, for starters, with so many letters that look familiar at first—look like a rho or a capital eta, for instance—that turn out to be very different. And just learning English is not quite enough, as every American high school student confronted with Macbeth discovers. It would take more study to be able to read Shakespeare's English. But those of us who love Shakespeare would say it was a noble effort of my Greek counterpart.

Effort is the key word here. I know I'll never read Homer with the same relative ease as I read Shakespeare. But I may come closer to that than I will to bulging biceps and six-pack abs from working out in the gym. Yet my wife will tell you that I go to the gym almost every day. And it turns out that the gym isn't a bad place to study Greek.

1.

I have never been a jock or an exercise-lover, but I became a regular at the gym after my second back operation. Some form of daily exercise became necessary to prevent my back from aching or going into spasm. So I joined a gym in Tucson, and went regularly for a few months. Then one day I showed up at the gym to find the doors locked and a sign saying they'd gone out of business—folded. I had given them my money up front, and, although I'd used the gym for a while, I still had a few bonus months left on my contract. But ουδέν κακόν αμιγές καλού: never evil unmixed with good. My wife suggested the Silver Sneakers program. I remembered vaguely that my health insurer subscribed to this program, but I'd thought it had something to do with exercise classes--not my cup of tea. Not so. I discovered I could sign up at any gym that belonged to the program—for free—and use the gym as a regular member. But that wasn't all. I could use any and all gyms in the program.

I promptly joined a gym open 24/7 that, though not close, is a quick drive out I-10 to the northwest. It's clean, there are plenty of treadmills and an array of leg and arm machines I like, and its lack of locker room facilities does not bother me; I don't wear special outfits or shower at the gym. I wear street clothes and have a low-impact routine—40 minutes' brisk walk and one set of 10 or 15 reps on each of half a dozen machines—that does not leave me sweaty or unsuited to get back on the street. But I do it every day.

I looked at the list of participating gyms and found to my surprise that the Tucson Racquet Club's fitness center is on it. The Racquet Club is an old Tucson institution at the end of Country Club Road where it runs into the Rillito River. I couldn't resist the impulse to join there, too. And finally I joined the YMCA downtown on Alameda. I had the city covered: east, northwest, and downtown.

The experience in these gyms is very different. The downtown Y has a clientele that reflects the make-up of the city, about half Mexican-American and half Anglo. The Y reminds me of my old gym, located in a barrio on Prince Road, where Saturday mornings smelled like the peppers and chickens roasting on the outdoor grill at El Herradero Market next door. Nothing is cooking at the Y, and it's cleaner and better equipped than my old gym, but I like the urban feel of the Y's basement exercise rooms and indoor track.

The Racquet Club is pretty Anglo by contrast, although one can see an occasional brown face. Like all gyms, this one has its muscle boys, but a lot of the stair-steppers and treadmills are occupied by women of two distinct ages. There are young women in their teens or twenties, many of whom clearly spend time on the courts as well and for whom exercise appears to be as natural as breathing. And then there are women of a certain age, working hard to outrun, if not the Angel of Death, at least the Demon of Gravity.

The northwest gym occupies a part of town where growth is fastest. The newest machines can be found there, as well as the most television sets, including big overhead screens and a small private set on each treadmill. The clientele is varied: a few retirees are always present, but younger men and women, some apparently taking a lunch hour or other short break from work, bustle in, do a hard workout, and bustle out. The gym sits in the middle of a suburban strip mall, and a few BMWs and Lexuses salt its mixture of family sedans and the ubiquitous Tucson open Jeep with roll bars and sheepskin seat-covers.

2.

At the beginning I had the wishful thought there might be an easy way to learn Greek, so I bought Peter Jones's *Learn Ancient Greek* and worked my way through a few chapters. Jones does indeed give you some of the feel of the language, and he entertains you while he's doing it; the subtitle of his book is *A Lively Introduction to Learning the Language*. He's done the same thing with his other popular book *Learn Latin*. The Latin book may be somewhat more successful than the Greek, just because Latin is closer to us English speakers. Greek is a complex language that requires some discipline just to master the alphabet. Another way to state the problem is to point to the fullness of Greek's inflection.

Like modern European languages, Greek *inflects* or modifies the endings of words to show their function in sentences. Every noun has a gender that must be learned.

Word endings indicating function, grouped into verb conjugations and noun/adjective declensions, have to be memorized. Greek's complexity includes not just singulars and plurals but an additional number: the *dual*. Where English has two voices, active and passive, Greek has a third: the *middle voice*.

Studying Greek starts with learning an unfamiliar alphabet. Pronunciation is no more difficult than in most European tongues but there is a system of accents that shift position relative to long vowels. Beginning and ending letters are added or changed, depending on adjacent words. Compare the way English modifies the pronunciation of *the* before a vowel or changes *a* to *an* in the same situation. While I'm still reading Peter Jones's book on Greek with pleasure, I knew I was going to have to have a little more system and rigor in my learning method to get very far with this language. An actual classroom course wasn't a practical idea for me. I spend part of the year in a little town where the college—Murray State University—does not offer Greek, and while Tucson, where I live the rest of the time, has a full Classics department at the University of Arizona, my irregular schedule means I'm seldom in town for a full semester.

A mail order business called The Teaching Company has a Greek course among its offerings. The Teaching Company hires professors who have distinguished teaching careers to record instructional CDs and DVDs on their subjects, marketing these impressively-produced home courses of study as *The Great Courses*. The instructor on my 36-lesson DVD course entitled *Greek 101: Learning an Ancient Language* is Hans-Friedrich Mueller, head of the Classics Department at Union College in Schenectady (Mueller also has a Teaching Company version of *Latin 101*). Mueller is a stocky, Ohio-born son of first-generation immigrants from Germany, with a huge shock of hair not always completely in control, though he is otherwise impeccably groomed and often wears a natty, double-breasted suit in these lectures. Each lesson is a half-hour in length and well-packed with material—but of course I can replay a lecture as often as I wish while working through its material.

After the alphabet and the system of accents comes the nitty-gritty of grammar. So far, in the order it has been presented by Dr. Mueller, I've learned about first-declension nouns, present-tense verbs, second-declension nouns, first and second declension adjectives, demonstrative, relative, and personal pronouns, the imperfect tense, the future tense, and the aorist tenses (roughly corresponding to English simple past)—and there is still more than half of the course to go. With these lessons go vocabulary words, up to several hundred by now. The only way to learn this stuff is to memorize it: the paradigms or models that show how a verb tense is formed or a noun or adjective is modified in different cases, and of course the vocabulary words: each noun along with an article that shows the gender of the noun plus a representative ending that shows its declension, the verbs with their six principal parts that give a shorthand key to the way their forms vary among the tenses, and so on through the other parts of speech. I use vocabulary cards to help me memorize, and for months now I've carried a small rubber-banded pack of them in my pocket, the selection of words changing from week to week.

My instructor, Dr. Mueller, frequently makes comments about the mental advantages of the memorization necessary to learn Greek, and how the recognition of pattern in endings makes the task easier. He is an engaging and striking fellow, with a brand of dry and understated humor. Though he teaches, as I've said, from DVD discs reproduced in the thousands for sale to Great Courses customers, it is as if he were talking directly to me when he makes these comments about the mental exercise of studying Greek. "Courage, μαθεται," he says, using the word that means both *students* and, in the Greek New Testament, *disciples*, "there is merit in repetition. Chant these endings aloud. Find the pattern." W. S. Merwin would agree; in "Learning a Dead Language" he writes, "You will find that that order helps you to remember."

3.

Treadmills at the downtown Y each have a deep reading shelf where a fat batch of Greek vocabulary cards will sit securely, and it's wide enough so I can spread the cards out into groups as I move through them, isolating the ones that have paradigms and the ones I believe I already know so I can concentrate on the others. The 24-hour gym in the suburbs, in addition to playing mindless music much too loud, has treadmills with a reading tray too shallow for my purposes—here one is expected to stare at one of the many TVs rather than read. The racquet club treadmills don't really have a reading shelf, but only a tray, often sticky, at the inconvenient level of the grab bars.

There's a rhythm I establish at the Y, which is unique among these gyms in having a small track that circles the weight room. Walking this track, perhaps with a couple of hand weights for some arm exercise, is a nice punctuation of my fifteen-minute turns on the treadmill. That length of time is just right to go through a stack of thirty or forty vocabulary cards in one direction—that is, reading the Greek side and coming up with the English translation. It's a little slower when I go the other way, because working out the spelling of the Greek word together with its gender if it's a noun or its odd forms if a verb takes more time than the simple recall of the English equivalent.

4.

Culture of body and mind is very Greek, but I don't fantasize about training for the umpteenth Olympiad or walking the Agora in dispute with philosophers. I have no test or contest in view with either my physical exercise activity—I could hardly call it a program—or the mental exercise of learning Greek vocabulary and trying to parse my way through one of Homer's sentences.

According to the National Institutes for Health study groups on aging and dementia, we don't really know exactly what kinds of mental activity such as puzzles, general reading, or games, for examples, may be most useful in giving the brain the same sort of workout with benefits such as regular exercise gives the body. We do know of evidence that *structured* cognitive activity, such as memory training, improves mental skills in older subjects, and the improvement lasts. Memorization has the structured features that have been found beneficial. We also know that physical exercise is good for the brain.

Not such good news for me is that *social* activity may be just as effective, or even more effective, in improving cognitive function in old guys like me, while my Greek study is essentially asocial: there isn't a conversational component to my language learning, and I'm just off by myself (even though often in a gym full of people) trying to remember words. I can't imagine anyone—except perhaps Hugh Lawson—that I might enlist as a study buddy in my odd project.

I am just trying to keep moderately fit so neither the mental wheels nor the corporal joints will seize up before the inevitable time of their dissolution. I don't even know whether the mental stretching of manipulating these unfamiliar letter forms makes any other thinking easier, but I know I believe in exercise. In moderation, of course. All in good measure. Παν μέτρον άριστον.

Playing Golf *versus* Reading About It

Bill Matthews has a poem, "Foul Shots: A Clinic," that talks about how instructions like standing "perpendicular to the basket" are "already…perilously abstract" and how other advice about making the shot can "grow spiritual" and probably deserves to be ignored. There's no substitute for just shooting 200 foul shots every single day. I know he's right, and that the point carries over to other games. Mine is golf. And I have read plenty of golf books. The first one I read, Tommy Armour's *How to Play Your Best Golf All the Time* (1953), really did teach me something about playing golf, but I had just picked up a club and any advice about grip and stance and swing could only be useful. The Silver Scot scolds his readers for not realizing that golf is a simple game, an assertion that is repeated by many writers—Arnold Palmer is one—but is irritating to high-handicap players. Golf books can be useful beyond any specific instructions if they encourage a player to think about what she is doing. Bobby Jones famously said that golf is a game played on a five-inch course: the distance between your ears. A thinking golfer will always beat a non-thinker of equal athletic ability.

The titles of the most famous golf instruction books tell us a great deal about the people who wrote them and their attitudes toward the game. Tommy Armour's title puts the emphasis on you, the reader. *Bobby Jones on Golf* (1966) suggests the talented amateur writing about one of the things he liked to do. Arnold Palmer's *My Game and Yours* (1965) manages to give the optimistic idea that some of Arnie's prodigious confidence and mastery might be transferable to the hacker. But Ben Hogan's book is forbiddingly called *Five Lessons: The Modern Fundamentals of Golf* (1957) and is illustrated with analytical drawings convincing me that unless I had been built like Hogan I couldn't master the very technical aspects of his swing. With Jack Nicklaus's *Golf My Way* (1974) we may be reminded that he is, so far, the greatest player who's ever competed; I have to ask, how can I possibly make his way my way? And finally, Tiger Woods's title is simply *How I Play Golf* (2001). A ghostly subtitle seems to glow under it: Do you really think *you* can do this? Some writers are a little more inviting. Corey Pavin, one of the half-dozen most inventive shotmakers in golf's history, calls his book *Shotmaking* (1996). Nick Faldo takes the long view of why you're playing in *A Swing for Life* (1995). Many of these books use almost identical words to describe the easy pressure you should use to grip the club, the temperate speed you must use to take the club back, and yes, how simple the game is. No one adds that it is simple only if you hit 200 range balls every single day.

Advice on Writing Your Suicide Note

1.

The suicide note, regardless of its mortal intent, is a piece of writing, and as in any other, the usual questions and choices have to be considered. The first question is always one of audience. Can you be sure that you are not attempting to defend your self-murder (let us be blunt while trying to avoid judgment) to the casual passer-by? The police may make up part of your reading audience; have you anything special to say to them? Or are you thinking that your loved ones are your most important readers, and that they are the ones you must convince that they bear no responsibility for your action and that, despite the fact that you love them dearly, you have decided to remove yourself from them violently? Bluntness again, but aren't these in fact your purposes: providing a reason for your action, giving the assurance that no one but you bears any responsibility for your act, and stressing the reminder that you love them?

With these notions about audience and intent, let us consider an example. The English actor George Sanders left a suicide note that read "Dear World, I am leaving because I am bored. I feel I have lived long enough. I am leaving you with your worries in this sweet cesspool. Good luck." Almost everything goes wrong with this note, beginning with the problem about audience: "Dear World" has become a comic stock opening for suicide notes, as cartoon characters about to flush themselves down a toilet begin their messages this way. Characteristically, Sanders underplays the performance in his last role, the part that is intended for the public. Apparently, depression alternated in his last days not with boredom, but with rage. The note conceals rather than explains. And the jocular, ironic tone is not quite successful, either. The question of tone has to be considered quite as carefully as any other. Adopting a jocular tone might seem to be consoling for those left behind, reassuring them about your attitude as you prepared to dispatch yourself. But you must consider your readers, who are apt to be in a state that will prevent them from appreciating humor, even of the subacid variety. Readers will assume despair on your part, and that you may be trying to mask it. If you are not despairing, the absence of despair may require more of an effort at explanation; that is, if you are not despairing, what is the point of the whole exercise?

2.

In fiction, suicide notes can be succinct ("Done because we are too menny" writes Old Father Time before he kills his siblings and himself in *Jude the Obscure*) and in a very different sense from those in real life, successful. All we ask of them there is that they convey the pathos and uselessness of the act and indignation at its causes.

But even the most adept of writers may not succeed when the note is outside of her fiction. We might look at Virginia Woolf's suicide note as an example of the problems of the genre. In several ways it is the perfect suicide note. And yet, it fails in what are clearly its main rhetorical purposes. Woolf's suicide note explains her actions adequately to anyone who knows the history to which she refers:

> Dearest, I feel certain that I am going mad again. I feel we can't go through another of those terrible times. And I shouldn't recover this time. I begin to hear voices, and I can't concentrate. So I am doing what seems the best thing to do.

Of course, Leonard Woolf might well have disputed his wife's conviction that she would not recover this time. In this sense the explanation is inadequate; it will never convince. The problem is inherent in all explanation of "why I did it." The explanation may be unnecessary (the ones left behind are aware of incurable physical illness in some cases; in others they are usually aware of severe mental illness and depression), it will probably be inadequate (the loved one will never be convinced that the suicide could not have been prevented with closer supervision, for example, or that the insanity or depression was irrecoverable), and it may be impossible, in the sense that the despair of the suicidal person is ineffable.

Given the obstacles of the first rhetorical purpose of explanation why the suicide acted, the most difficult rhetorical challenge that remains is convincing the loved one who reads the note that he or she bears no responsibility and that the act, regardless of its violent and apparently hostile nature, is not meant to deny that the suicide genuinely loves the reader. Consider how Virginia Woolf carefully repeats and restates the issue in addressing her husband:

> You have given me the greatest possible happiness. You have been in every way all that anyone could be. I don't think two people could have been happier 'til this terrible disease came. I can't fight any longer. I know that I am spoiling your life, that without me you could work. And you will I know. You see I can't even write this properly. I can't read. What I want to say is I owe all the happiness of my life to you. You have been entirely patient with me and incredibly good. I want to say that—everybody knows it. If anybody could have saved me it would have been you. Everything has gone from me but the certainty of your goodness. I can't go on spoiling your life any longer. I don't think two people could have been happier than we have been. V.

These iterated phrases are exquisitely painful; we can feel her straining to assure him that no lack of love or attention on his part could possibly in any way have contributed to her action. And yet, can we believe that he was convinced? He may indeed have never wavered in his love, but he could not be with her every minute. He was not there at the precise minute she filled her overcoat pockets with stones and walked into the River Ouse.

3.

When David Foster Wallace committed suicide in 2008, he left a note to his wife Karen Green. We'll probably never see it. But as Benjamin Alsup wrote in a review of Wallace's posthumously-published novel *The Pale King*, when a writer commits suicide he invites us to read all of his previous work as one long suicide note. Wallace did talk about suicide, not just in his fiction. In a commencement address he gave at Kenyon College in 2005, three years before his death, Wallace warns the graduands about solipsism, which he calls the mind's default setting:

> everything in my own immediate experience supports my deep belief that I am the absolute center of the universe; the realest, most vivid and important person in existence. We rarely think about this sort of natural, basic self-centeredness because it's so socially repulsive. But it's pretty much the same for all of us. It is our default setting, hard-wired into our boards at birth. Think about it: there is no experience you have had that you are not the absolute center of. The world as you experience it is there in front of YOU or behind YOU, to the left or right of YOU, on YOUR TV or YOUR monitor. And so on. Other people's thoughts and feelings have to be communicated to you somehow, but your own are so immediate, urgent, real.

Wallace enjoins his listeners to try to stay in touch with the reality that denies this self-absorption because, he says, if they cannot, they "will be totally hosed."

> Think of the old cliché about "the mind being an excellent servant but a terrible master." This, like many clichés, so lame and unexciting on the surface, actually expresses a great and terrible truth. It is not

the least bit coincidental that adults who commit suicide with firearms almost always shoot themselves in the head. They shoot the terrible master. And the truth is that most of these suicides are actually dead long before they pull the trigger.

Wallace did not shoot himself in the head; he hanged himself. Given the vigilance of Wallace's parents (who took care of him when his wife had to be away) and of his wife toward his state of mind in his last months of life, it is unlikely that there would have been any firearms in his house. The anti-depression medication Wallace had been taking for several decades had stopped working, and doctors were trying to deal with his depression with other therapies and other medications.

4.

Wallace's words help make it clear why the effort to explain the act of suicide can be so futile. The prison house of the individual mind, the "default" setting of solipsism, the closed loop of thought which never gets beyond the self, these are in the depressed person's mind exaggerated; the result is being unable to think about the world outside it as being continuous with the enclosed mind rather than completely other or hardly existing. In this mental state, the effort to explain the act of suicide is futile from the start. "They are not inside my mind; therefore they cannot understand." Our examples seem to point to the impossibility of communicating the reasons, the impossibility of justification. And this impossibility raises several questions. Does the futility become obvious in the act of writing a suicide note, and has a potential suicide ever turned aside from the act when the attempt to justify it showed itself as impossible? It seems unlikely that once the note stage is reached, that turning back is possible. "Suicide is painless," goes the song in Robert Altman's *M*A*S*H*. "It brings on many changes, and I can take or leave it if I please." Only the second of these assertions seems to be invariably true, regardless of

Wallace's comment about the suicides who are actually dead before they pull the trigger.

But the most fundamental question is, why are you writing a suicide note at all? It may seem obvious from the discussion so far that your purposes are to explain why you are acting and to try to deflect guilt from those left behind while assuring them that you love them. Yet a note is not only a very imperfect way to do these things, but a very impersonal one. Why not a face-to-face discussion? Perhaps because you know already that you aren't going to convince them that the situation is irredeemable. Moreover, they may ask the uncomfortable question of why you don't refrain from doing this precisely because you do love them. Thus, with the fundamental question comes a glimpse into the fundamental impossibility in writing a suicide note that successfully explains and reassures.

5.

If you have faith in the written word you may not wish to believe it won't work here. Aren't there precedents for a written communication accomplishing what couldn't be accomplished in a face-to-face one? How about D'Arcy's letter to Eliza Bennet explaining why he acted as he did? It eventually does a pretty good job of getting her to come around to D'Arcy's point of view, while everything he said while he was proposing just had the effect of making her angrier and more scornful of his way of seeing things. Of course, D'Arcy hung around long enough for Eliza to wish to be reconciled. The suicide, on the other hand, is no longer available. Suicide is, among other things, a rhetorical act that says two things with no possibility of rejoinder from those you leave behind: that succeeding in explaining things to them is not necessary, and that your love for them will not impede you from acting. Suicide is the denial of communication, its final cut-off. To suppose that the note can somehow explain away the monstrous implications of the act is to have too much faith in rhetoric.

6.

Suicides sometimes act with the complete agreement of their loved ones, in a situation—almost always a terminal illness—where all parties have agreed cessation of life is the best thing. When we hear that a note has been left behind, we can guess that that agreement was not reached. It is thus a doomed genre of writing practiced by a doomed author. No one can give us instruction in this genre.

Dorothy Parker, though she attempted suicide two or three or four times—depending on whom one consults as a source—famously addressed the difficulties of suicide in her poem "Résumé," though she had nothing to say about the difficulty of writing the notes. She runs through the inconvenience, messiness, and possible failure of various suicide methods, and she concludes "You might as well live." Parker at last took her own advice.

A Chance Conversation

Lately, I have been trying to think through the idea of contingency. By contingency, I mean the causal dependence of one event upon another, which leads us to the related idea of chance—the chance of something happening versus the chance of nothing or of anything else happening. An essay of the sort you are reading, written by someone who is not a household name and submitted "over the transom," has less than one chance in twenty of being accepted by a magazine, according to my experience. For the magazine essay to be collected with others and find a book publisher is chancier still. It seems like a very small chance that you and I met like this.

And yet it is in the nature of historical contingency that it bears the appearance of inevitability. The careers of great military leaders offer good examples. Take Horatio Nelson. To reach the pinnacle of military success he occupied at the time he was shot down at the Battle of Trafalgar, Nelson had to have survived previous battles in which he showed the same disdain for danger by exposing himself to enemy fire. Moreover, he had to have been successful each time he was in charge, and success in such endeavors does not always depend on superior forces or ability. His rivals in the British Navy had, meanwhile, to be less conspicuously successful. Nelson had only one eye and one arm left by the time of Trafalgar, and he was a walking illustration of how lucky he was to be alive, let alone to have prevailed so often. Yet we have the impression in reading his story that Nelson willed himself to greatness. Well, in a sense he did, but it was chance and contingency that ensured that his willfulness was not cut off, with his life, along the way.

A fictional character like Shakespeare's Iago seems to have an inevitability about him—to be unstoppable—while in fact it is precisely because he runs a moment-by-moment danger of being destroyed that his character is so fascinating. Alexandre Dumas says of his delightfully villainous Milady de Winter, "Great criminals bear about them a kind of predestination which makes them surmount all obstacles, which makes them escape all dangers, up to the moment which a wearied Providence has marked as the rock of their impious fortunes." But it is not predestination; it is a willingness to court every dangerous chance and a series of such chances coming up favorably until the last inevitable one goes the wrong way. At which point we say that Providence grew tired of our villain.

*

I have trouble getting my head around certain aspects of chance, especially the harsher parts: One could have never been at all; one could cease being at any instant. That third-person construction in the last two clauses is a clue to how tender the thought is of not-being. What I avoided writing was that there could just as easily never have been me; at any instant there could cease to be me. Because I know that it can be hard to think about such matters, I have always liked writers who tackled the difficulties of chance and contingency. Those who do so can even be imagined as in a conversation with one another.

The easier idea is that of death: We will all at some unknowable time cease existing. Children learn about death, and they begin to think that their parents might die—a frightening thought—and that they themselves might die—a thought probably more puzzling than scary at first. Eventually, they understand that every living thing dies.

Virginia Woolf is the writer who seems to me to have most successfully tackled the issue of what happens when the human presence suddenly becomes an absence. In one of her early books, *Jacob's Room*, even though Jacob appears in the book—as a child, as an undergraduate, as a young man—and even though we read his thoughts occasionally, the book is really about the room Jacob takes up in other people's consciousness. He is pictured as he is thought of by others, some of them strangers: "One must do the best one can with her report," Woolf writes of a woman who sees him only in the train down to Cambridge and never again.

Jacob's Room and *To the Lighthouse* are un-English in an important sense—books out of the tradition that self-consciousness is how a novelist goes after a character. Both of these books have an ancient Greek literary quality in affirming that what we are, our identity, is very much a product of how we affect others. It's more complicated than how we appear to others, though that is a part of it. In any case, we are not what we imagine ourselves to be. Jacob's room at Trinity College is described, as is his room in London, and this literal sense is also part of what the book is about: Jacob is partly what he surrounds himself with, in the way of things or people or chosen experience. The main sense of the title, though, is the space Jacob occupies in the world and the minds of those who encounter him, as well as the absence he leaves when he's dead. There are plenty of signals throughout that indicate that the book is moving toward Jacob's absence: Descriptions end with graveyards or poppies; one begins, "The lamps of London uphold the dark as upon the points of burning bayonets"; and a would-be romance concludes, "And now Jimmy feeds crows in France and Helen visits hospitals." But the dates and even Jacob's last name ought to lead us to suspect how the novel will end. "Jacob Flanders, therefore, went up to Cambridge in October, 1906," Woolf writes, and of course this puts him in his mid-twenties when the Great War begins and possibly in Flanders fields when it ends.

In *To the Lighthouse*, we barely have time to realize how important Mrs. Ramsay is to the well-being of all around her when Woolf suddenly announces her death. Then we get to see how things do not hold together without the linchpin she provided. The only character in the book who sees how vital Mrs. Ramsay was, the artist Lily Briscoe, liked to chide the older woman for her old-fashioned ideas of women's places. But Lily realizes that Mrs. Ramsay arranged the world around her "like a work of art." She brought people together; she created harmony, "making of the moment something permanent" in a way Lily would like to do with her painting.

*

Of course, the real theater of contingency is one's own experience. We all know our lives could have been very different, suddenly or over the course of years, but for some chances.

Early one summer morning when he was twenty-five, my son Dan woke us with a telephone call from Johnson City, Tennessee, near the border with North Carolina. Dan was in a hospital emergency room after being flown by a Medevac helicopter from an accident on Interstate 40. Dan had stopped at the scene and walked toward a car that had been hit head-on by a pickup truck going the wrong way on the interstate. Dan approached the car, which was in the passing lane and facing the side of the road. He walked around the car and up to the driver's side window to see if he could help, and, at that moment, a semi-trailer truck, going the right way on the freeway, hit the car from the other side. Dan was thrown thirty feet across the highway median, and he was unconscious until the paramedics woke him.

Miraculously, he had no concussion, no broken bones, and no internal injuries. His eyeglasses had disappeared, and gradually he would see huge bruises develop that would highlight where his belt and the buttons of his shirt had been. He had been driving a rental car, which was towed from the scene and was now in a salvage yard, its battery dead. Dan had turned on the emergency blinkers when he pulled off the road; the semi driver, seeing the flashing lights, had moved into the passing lane to avoid the stopped car with its blinkers flashing and had hit the unlit car there before he could stop.

Unfortunately, such after-accidents are not uncommon. One of them crippled the writer Andre Dubus, but the usual outcome is the death of the Good Samaritan. As my wife and I drove toward Johnson City on I-40, we looked carefully for signs of the accident we knew had occurred somewhere in that stretch of road. Nothing marked the spot, an unmemorable place on the interstate, but we both had the same thought: It would have been memorable enough that we would never have forgotten it as long as we lived, had things gone less fortunately for Dan.

*

We frequently speak of chance as being causative, an error that my gambling friends warn me against; there is no force operating more strongly on the coin to turn up heads after it has successively come up tails three times, four times, five times. Yet chance intervenes so often in what seems a mechanical thread of contingency that it affects all of us, however humble our circumstances. In fact, the existence of our species itself highlights the tenuousness of the thread of contingency. And this tenuousness forms a thread of the argument in Stephen Jay Gould's book *Wonderful Life: The Burgess Shale and the Nature of History* (1989). Gould describes the tiny Cambrian Period animals found in the Burgess Shale, a fossil-rich rock in the Colorado Rockies. Gould believes that the lesson of the Burgess Shale fauna, and also of the Luis Alvarez hypothesis—now generally accepted—that the great Cretaceous-Tertiary extinction resulted from the impact of an asteroid, is that history is contingent, resting on "an unpredictable sequence of antecedent states, where any major change in any step of the sequence would have altered the final result." All of the biologists and paleontologists who have recently examined the Burgess Shale fauna have acknowledged that "a contemporary observer could not have selected the organisms destined for success" in the group, and that, in Gould's words, the survival process was more like a lottery than a directed process.

Gould's frequent image is "replaying the tape"—that is, going back to some point such as the Cambrian Period and starting again. His contention is that the animals that survived would be different and the likelihood of the evolution of human intelligence extremely small. Moreover, he says, the very late appearance of human evolution, halfway through the cycle of our sun, suggests that if it had taken even twice as long, let alone ten or twenty times, it would have been too late. His statement about humans and contingency is "*Homo sapiens* is an entity, not a tendency, and far less an inevitability."

Our usual picture of natural selection, which I believe we form as an accommodation to the less thinkable parts of chance, is that the adapted creature survives and reproduces and therefore is preserved. But what if the adapted creatures, thriving in their little world, suddenly have a wall of mud fall on them, extinguishing them and literally flattening them as if they'd been run over by a truck? Their deaths—the end of their possibility of surviving to pass on their adaptation—are a part of natural selection we don't like to think about. Such a minor catastrophe created the Burgess Shale fossils. The great Cretaceous-Tertiary extinction took out a lot of well-adapted reptilian species and gave some little mammals a chance their mutations hadn't earned them. They survived Earth's equivalent of being hit by a truck, lived through the sunless winter caused by the impact's clouds of dust, and found themselves in a world with fewer predators and more room to reproduce and, of course, mutate.

We want things to be neater than this, with effects traceable to their causes, without random interruptions. We have what Wallace Stevens called a "rage for order." There is order, but it is oblivious to human concerns—or those of any other species, for that matter. Indeed, *matter* is the right word; the ineluctable is only at the level of matter and its behavior in what we call—invoking human institutions even in behavior that ignores the human—"laws" or "rules." The search for first causes leads us back, finally, to protons and other particles, gravity, electromagnetism, strong and weak forces.

*

My wife's favorite aunt married a geologist, a Spaniard who grew up in Caracas after his family was exiled during the Spanish Civil War. One day on his patio in the hills above Austin, Amos began telling me how he came to be a geologist. I realized that it was a story about the course of his life, including his marriage, and that, had it not gone this way, he would have been telling another story to quite another nephew-in-law.

Amos had planned on becoming an architect, like his father. He had heard that the best school was the University of Virginia, he had been admitted, and he was applying for a visa to go. But there had been a problem with his birth certificate, which had been lost as his family had fled Spain. Now, a martinet American Consulate bureaucrat kept him from getting the visa. And Amos ran into a high-school friend who said he should major in geology at the university in Caracas. "It's so much fun," the friend said, describing field trips, not-too-rigorous lab work, and meeting girls. Amos's future was decided by a recalcitrant paper-pusher and an eager rock-jock. He would eventually become a U. S. citizen and rise to be Chief Geologist for Exxon (no problem about visas any more), as well as, after retiring, one of the stars of the geology department at the University of Texas. Had it not been for the two chances of the bureaucrat and the friend, Amos would never have majored in geology, would never have gone to Stanford's graduate school, where he met his future wife, who was an undergraduate in a lab where he was the teaching assistant. He would never have been in the family; I would probably never have met him, let alone have heard this story from him.

Amos knew that one chance event—the bureaucrat whose passion for correct birth records kept Amos from attending the University of Virginia—did not establish the interlocking contingencies that put him where he was now. Every event is a result of a series of chances, and here there had been at least three: his diversion from architecture, his remaining in Caracas rather than going to the States as an undergraduate, and his move to geology.

*

I recently read Joseph Conrad's *Chance*. Though he had been writing for almost twenty years and had published a dozen books, Conrad had had no real popular or critical success until *Chance* was published in 1913. Then he had both, and his other works received the recognition they deserved, as well.

Conrad puts on the title page an epigraph from Sir Thomas Browne: "Those that hold that all things are governed by Fortune had not erred, had they not persisted there." The epigraph is oddly, ironically inconsistent with Conrad's narrative, in which everything seems overdetermined by chance, if such an oxymoronic way of putting it may be permitted.

The unnamed narrator of the story and Conrad's familiar character Marlow happen to meet a man named Charles Powell as they are cruising the mouth of the Thames, where Powell, now retired from the sea, likes to sail in his small cutter. Powell tells the two men the story of his first officer's berth, which he got when a friend threw a chance suggestion to him to go see a man at the shipping office who just happened to be named Powell as well, though he was no relation. While at the shipping office, Powell meets a captain, who just happens to have lost his second mate that very day to a carriage accident. Again, by chance, Marlow happens to know of this captain and his ship, or, to be more precise, he has met the girl, Flora de Barral, whom the captain once saved from suicide.

The conclusion of the story is quick and melodramatic: During "...a moonless night, thick with stars above, very dark on the water," Powell, looking by chance through the cabin skylight, sees a man poisoning the captain's drink. Later still, we learn that Flora now lives near the mouth of the Thames, where Powell likes to sail. Conrad seems here to be testing our willingness to believe by piling up coincidence, and indeed I am reminded of a remark E. M. Forster makes in *Aspects of the Novel*: that a novelist ought to put one big coincidence in his plot, because every reader knows that coincidence is a fact of life, but the author had better avoid any more than the one, because the reader also knows that coincidence is rare. In fact, Conrad is perfectly aware that he is piling it on, and his point seems to be that any meeting or parting, any new course of life, anything that happens to us, is a result of a series of chances. One of the many ways that chance works, one that's so obvious that we have to notice it, is coincidence.

*

In Arizona's Chiricahua Mountains last year, I was birding with some friends. Our guide, Tony Godfrey, had been a fireman for almost twenty years before he suddenly quit and became a nature guide. In one of Tony's stories about his firefighting days, he enters a building—a restaurant— where there is a fire, and in the dining room there is no flame. He and the two men with him punch a hole in the ceiling but find no flame there, either. They go into the kitchen and find fire only when they punch through the ceiling, but one of the three has difficulties with his oxygen tank, and all three go outside to fix it. As they reenter the dining room, another fireman, who has entered the kitchen from another door, issues a mayday call because an air conditioner unit on the roof is starting to come down, and he believes that the other firefighters are inside, in harm's way. The air conditioner crashes through the ceiling into the kitchen, the fire explodes through the ground floor, and Tony and the other two firemen are blown back out the door they have just re-entered. The delay with the oxygen tank has saved their lives.

*

In *The Maltese Falcon*, the detective Sam Spade talks about a man he was hired to search for in the Northwest, a man named Flitcraft, who had abandoned his wife and children to start a completely new life when a construction beam fell near him, and he realized how quickly and arbitrarily he could have been killed. The incident, he felt, "had taken the lid off life and let him look at the works, showing him that it was not the "clean orderly sane respectable affair" he had thought but one in which "men died at haphazard like that, and lived only while blind chance spared them." The part Spade likes best is that when nothing further happened of this revelatory or remarkable sort, Flitcraft settled into the same middle-class, suburban life he had left behind, with a new family almost identical to the one he had deserted.

Our guide Tony Godfrey reacted to his look at "the works" by giving up his job as a firefighter and starting a new life as a nature guide. Now, I could call that merely a reasonable assessment of the danger of his job, but he didn't just leave something behind; he asserted his own will. Francis Bacon writes in "Of Fortune" that, though we cannot deny that accidents contribute to our fate, yet "chiefly, the mould of a man's fortune is in his own hands."

When I think about my life, my family, and my friends, I am inclined to tot up the interventions of chance as fortunate ones. But I do not wish to tempt any "purblind Doomsters," as Thomas Hardy writes in "Hap," to change the balance. What I do wish is that I could get Browne and Woolf, Bacon and Gould, Conrad and Hardy together for a discussion about chance and contingency. Perhaps the discussion is going on right now, and it's just my luck to be missing it.

Paris from the Terrace

The terrorists of November 2015 tried to attack an essential of Paris life—the café scene and especially the terrace cafés. Thinking of what these Parisian institutions have meant to me, I imagine a walk through the city, stopping at a few of the cafés, and conjuring up the books about Paris the walk would evoke. Let's begin at La Closerie des Lilas on the Boulevard du Montparnasse near where the Boulevard Saint-Michel begins. I took my family to eat here the last time we were all in Paris. A. J. Liebling used to stop here for a drink after a workout at his boxing gym nearby. Liebling's *Between Meals* (1959) is one of my favorite books about Paris. Liebling spent the year 1926-27 supposedly studying in Paris, and he returned as a correspondent from 1939 until shortly before Paris fell. He came back in with the liberation, visited again right after the war and again in 1948. He made several visits during the fifties before the writing of this book. He records his memories of the city, her sporting clubs, one particular fellow-glutton (a minor playwright named Yves Mirande), and one particular prostitute named Angéle. But mostly the memories are of food, wine, cognac, Calvados, and restaurants. In one memorable meal, Liebling and Mirande began with *truite bleu* followed by two meat courses (because they could not make up their minds): a *daube Provençale* and *pintadous* or guinea hens. An Alsatian Sainte Odile accompanied the fish, a Pétrus the *daube*, and a Cheval Blanc the *pintadous*. They had three bottles of champagne after the meal.

Hemingway drank at the Closerie with Ford Madox Ford, among others. He lived in the street behind the restaurant in the 20s with his first wife, and he writes about it in *A Moveable Feast* (1964), another favorite. He writes about friendships with Gertrude Stein, Sylvia Beach (the owner of the bookstore Shakespeare and Company, which published Joyce's *Ulysses* in 1922), Ezra Pound, Scott and Zelda Fitzgerald, and many others. The book covers the years between 1921 and 1926, when Hemingway was writing *The Sun Also Rises* (1926), which begins in Paris and reflects in part Hemingway's life and associates during this time.

We could walk through the Luxembourg Gardens northward toward our next destination, Saint-Germain-des-Prés, but the Métro will take us there directly. And speaking of the Métro, the last book I read about Paris was Raymond Queneau's *Zazie in the Metro* (1959), about a twelve-year-old girl left by her mother in the care of her uncle Gabriel for the weekend. Zazie is foul-mouthed but fairly innocent; all she really wants to do in Paris is ride the Métro, but its workers are on strike. Gabriel, as Gabriella, does a ballerina parody of Swan Lake at a gay nightclub called the Mount of Venus, and the question of whether Gabriel himself is gay or not is one of the book's many ambiguities. Gabriel is married to the gentle Marceline, but she turns into the very male Marcel at the end, rescuing Gabriel's crowd at the Queen of the Night from ruffians and delivering Zazie back to her mother. Such reversals of sexual or other sorts of identity are reflected in reversals within the book's language, which is also full of Parisian slang, words run together or elided, puns and allusions of an almost Joycean plenitude. Barbara Wright's 1960 translation succeeds in Englishing all this admirably. Louis Malle made a movie of the book in 1960, but it does not capture the language's fireworks and is little but a frenetic romp through tourist views of Paris.

The center of the district of Saint-Germain-des-Prés is the corner of the Boulevard Saint-Germain and the Rue Bonaparte, with its numerous cafés, including the Café de Flore, where Raymond Queneau was a regular, as was Picasso. Its rival, Les Deux Magots, was a favorite of Hemingway and Joyce. From a table at Deux Magots, and from the official and artistic centers of the city, Janet Flanner told Americans what was happening in Paris in the thirties and what to think about it. Flanner's bi-weekly articles in

The New Yorker were collected as *Paris Was Yesterday 1925-1939* (1972). Her first entry in her first letter described Josephine Baker at the Théâtre des Champs-Élysées; her last was posted amid daily drills and air raid sirens a week before the invasion of Poland. In between she wrote about Paris nobility, performers such as Isadora Duncan, Marlene Dietrich, and Mae West, with many returns over the years to the career of Josephine Baker. She knew many art world figures and describes the funeral of Eugène Atget and conversations with Picasso. Politicians and military figures show up often, from the death of Marshal Foch in 1929 to the accession of Léon Blum as Premier in 1936.

In the nineties Adam Gopnik became the new Janet Flanner, reporting to *The New Yorker* from Paris, where he had moved with his family. His *From Paris to the Moon* (2000) weighs the relative popularity of Les Deux Magots and the Café de Flore in a discussion about French restaurants that bemoans the expense of some but says many, such as La Closerie des Lilas, Lapérouse (which Liebling thought had become terrible by the fifties), and Le Petit St. Benoît, are still good or are returning to favor among the knowing. Gopnik also writes about contemporary French philosophers, politics, and haute couture.

To the west of these cafés is the Faubourg Saint-Germain, historically the neighborhood of French nobility and containing the homes to whose fictional counterparts Proust's Charles Swann was accustomed to be admitted. Throughout *In Search of Lost Time* (1913-27), Proust's Paris never has the detail he gives to walks in Combray or to the beaches of Balbec. In Proust's Paris the action is indoors.

In any case we are bound in the other direction, down the Boulevard Saint-Germain and its many shops to the Boulevard Saint-Michel. Along the way we pass one of the offices of the Alliance Française—perhaps the one David Sedaris attended. In *Me Talk Pretty One Day* (2000), Sedaris hilariously describes his attempts to learn French as an adult in a Paris language school, with his fellow students from all over the globe struggling along with him.

Turn left at the Boulevard Saint-Michel and a short walk takes us to the Place Saint-Michel, the very heart of Paris, at least the heart of the literary ex-pats' Paris. Here Hemingway often worked in a clean, well-lighted café. The Place shows up in Maugham, Joyce, Zora Neale Hurston, and a dozen other writers besides Hemingway. A few steps away, in the Place Saint-André des Arts, I found a 5th floor walkup hotel room where I crashed during April of my 21st year while I explored Paris.

Just across the bridge that crosses the Seine from the Place Saint-Michel is the Île de la Cité, where Eugène Sue's *The Mysteries of Paris* (1842-43) begins. Sue's work was a tremendous popular success first as a serial and then in book form, and it spawned a whole genre of writing about the underside of great cities of the world. An unabridged English translation—1400 pages long—has just become available from Penguin.

The Île is only a couple of blocks wide, and if we continue we cross the Seine again. Left along the quay a few blocks takes us to the Louvre, where Henry James's Christopher Newman meets Noémie Nioche copying one of the museum's masterpieces in *The American* (1877). Newman tries, as do many of James's Americans, to woo the Old World and take it home with him, but he fails, as do they, and ends up sadder and wiser.

Around the corner from the Louvre, just off the Rue de Rivoli is the theater of the Comédie Française, at the bottom of the Avenue de l'Opéra. Here Cornelia Otis Skinner, an aspiring actress, took lessons and attended performances several times a week. She and her friend Emily Kimbrough were newly graduated from Bryn Mawr and abroad for the first time in the 1920s. They did not collaborate on their account of their trip, *Our Hearts Were Young and Gay*, until 1942. A hipper and sexier version of the young girl goes to Paris is Elaine Dundy's novel, *The Dud Avocado* (1958). A randy young American girl on an extended trip to Paris financed by her rich uncle tells us of her love affairs, her disillusionment with Europeans, her disillusionment with Americans, and so on.

Were we to walk northwest along the Rue de Rivoli, we would eventually reach the Place de la Concorde, the location of the infamous "Hotel X" where the young Eric Blair worked long hours as a *plongeur*, the lowest of the kitchen help, in the hotel restaurant. As George Orwell, he wrote about it in his first book, *Down and Out in Paris and London* (1933). But if we go the other way down the Rue de Rivoli, we will soon find ourselves in the Marais, historically the Jewish quarter of Paris. This neighborhood is the scene of Cara Black's first mystery of many set in the various quartiers of Paris. Black's detective, Aimée Leduc, is spike-haired, with jeans, leather jacket and boots. She is the daughter of a *flic*, a Parisian policeman, and his American wife who bolted when Aimée was eight years old—we don't know why, but I suspect someone corrected her French pronunciation one time too many. The Marais and the Rue de Louvre, where Leduc has her office and the Île Saint-Louis, where Aimée has inherited an apartment from her grandfather, form the backdrops for this mystery, which has its beginnings in Nazi-occupied Paris, but is very much about the city and its people in the nineties. This book shows us Paris from the rooftops to the catacombs and the sewers. Aimée Leduc's creator, Cara Black, is not French but American, but this sort of cultural appropriation is common in detective fiction, where you will find another Parisian detective, Maigret, created by a Belgian, a Belgian detective, Poirot, created by an Englishwoman, and English, Irish, and Italian detectives all created by Americans. And the original fictional detective, the Chevalier C. Auguste Dupin, was also a Parisian created by the American Edgar Allan Poe.

Of course, there are as many good books about Paris as there are streets and cafés in the city, but I suspect that by this time you are pretty thirsty and it's time to stop. Here's a place, Le Gribouille, on the Rue de Rivoli, where we can watch the passersby. Probably no one has written a book about it yet. Perhaps we can celebrate it in our own scribbles while we have a vermouth cassis or an express. Or better yet, a glass of Suresne, a true Parisian wine made in its environs.

Brillat-Savarin expressed his contempt for Suresne in *The Physiology of Taste* (1825). It is earthy, cheap, mediocre, and completely drinkable; here, on this Paris street, drinking it is practically a statement of defiance. Terroir versus terror.

The Road to Beatrice

The last stretch of road into my wife's hometown of Beatrice, Nebraska is the eventful little two-lane State Highway 136 that leads from I-29 north of St. Joseph, Missouri into Beatrice. Beatrice, by the way, was the birthplace of the actor Robert Taylor (though the locals knew him as Spangler Arlington Brugh) and the poet Weldon Kees (whom the locals called Weldie). When I say the locals I mean my mother-in-law, who has lived in Beatrice all her life.

Turning west from I-29 onto 136, you come almost immediately to a bridge that will take you into Brownville. (If you are coming from St. Louis, this will be the third time you cross the Missouri River). Often the center of these little towns is worth the out-of-the-way few blocks you must go to reach it, and Brownville is no exception. Technically a village of fewer than 150 souls, Brownville boasts some fine historic buildings on Main Street, and on the river, a floating bed and breakfast. A few miles farther west is Auburn, which always calls to my mind the opening couplet of Goldsmith's "The Deserted Village":

> Sweet Auburn! Loveliest village of the plain,
> Where health and plenty cheer'd the laboring swain....

Unlike Brownville, Auburn is not a village but a city of 3500. Its first sign is an airport where there are two intersecting turf runways, the only one of its kind I've seen. Auburn's graveyard is on the highway and called Sheridan Cemetery, but as we leave the city we find its annex: on rolling turf easy to mistake for a golf course a very few headstones are visible, and gates that proclaim this as "Sheridan West."

Not much farther, at Spring Creek, you'll see a working bison farm, with its feed lot and pasture wrapped around a house on the south side of the road. The last time I passed there were dozens of buffalo within a few yards of the highway, a startling sight more common on these plains two hundred years ago. The next creeks form an interesting contrast of names. The first is Brewer's Branch, calling up for me southern associations of "branch water" that always seems to be linked to alcohol—paired with bourbon or used for brewing. But the next crossing is Yankee Creek.

Almost immediately we are in Tecumseh, where we do one of those mysterious ninety-degree turns followed by another ninety-degree turn back to course a few blocks later; this is a fairly common occurrence in Midwest driving where roads avoid a parcel of land some farmer resisted giving up to the right of way. And the next town is Beatrice.

What strikes an observer about the streets of this town is the number of trees throughout the city. They are more numerous than in any other of the towns spread across southeastern Nebraska. Yet the locals will tell you (my mother-in-law again) that before the advent of Dutch Elm Disease that killed almost all of the fine American Elms in Beatrice, there were twice as many trees here. Beatrice boasts the very first homestead, applied for shortly after midnight on the day Lincoln's 1862 *Homestead Act* went into effect. The Homestead National Monument is on the other side of town. To the north is Beatrice's airport, where you can depart on its runway 36 and fly straight without a course change the thirty-three nautical miles onto runway 36 at Lincoln. I know; I've done it.

South Texas Diary, 2006

And may the saints' blessings and grace
Carry me safely into your arms
There across the border.
—Bruce Springsteen, "Across the Border"

In 2006 my friend and colleague J. D. and I had been invited to housesit in South Texas. An old friend of mine from Tucson and his wife ran an elegant bed and breakfast that catered to nature lovers, especially birdwatchers, adjacent to a wildlife refuge right on the Rio Grande. Our job, while Trudy and Jim Taggart were away during the end of August and the beginning of September, was to keep the birdfeeders full and tend to the four dogs. All the cleaning and gardening for the five guest units and the separate main house were contracted out. The workers were all Spanish-speaking locals and J. D.'s impeccable Spanish would be handy, since the maid couldn't really speak much English. J. D. grew up in nearby Kingsville, and he has a postgraduate degree in Spanish, as well as the English degrees that brought him to the Kentucky college where we both taught. We flew into McAllen a day before the Taggarts were due to leave for their vacation.

The main house's patio, sheltered except for its view of the tree-lined boundary road, along which the only traffic was the occasional border patrol van, has a small pool and a fenced, grassy area so the dogs could be let out for less than a full run when they just needed a quick pee. Could we have turned this down? No, we couldn't.

Friday 8/25/06

The hummingbird feeders ranged across the back patio are getting a good number of visits. During most of the day there would be a Buff-bellied or a Ruby-throat at each feeder, and sometimes two or even three birds would show up at one feeder, twittering over the little modeled plastic flowers, pierced so that the tiny long bills could get at the sugar water. Hummingbirds are so competitive that we rarely saw four birds drinking from a feeder at the same time, though the feeder bottoms had four openings with perches beneath each one. Most of the time one bird won the dive-bombing and scolding contest, drank, and was buzzed or feinted from the feeder in turn.

Trudy showed us how to mix the hummingbird water in large-mouth gallon jugs with a mark at the level we were to fill the sugar. Two of these jugs lived in the refrigerator, where they were ready to fill the feeders, which held about a quart each. An entire drawer of feeder bottoms and a shelf of glass tops rotated with the four feeders hanging from the eaves outside.

Saturday 8/26/06

Up about seven and coffee while Jim and Trudy got ready to go. We drove them to the airport in the Expedition, stopped at McCreery Aviation for me to arrange a check ride, and then drove to the big HEB for barbacoa, tortillas, and a few other items. Lunch, pool, reading. Decided to eat in and had a chorizo omelet.

Sunday 8/27/06

To Our Lady of Sorrows on Hackberry in McAllen for mass. We drove past a house on that street that had belonged to J.D.'s aunt when he was growing up in the Valley. We went back to McAllen in the evening for dinner at a Thai restaurant. As we got out of the car, a flock of Red-fronted Parrots came flying in and circled us, cawing loudly, and then flew away.

Monday 8/28/06

Up to feed the dogs and off to pick up the lady who cleans—we got lost on the way and had to backtrack looking for the right road, but eventually found it. I left about 10 for the McAllen airport while J. D. went to the bosque to sit and watch birds. An old fellow at McCreery Aviation checked my credentials about four times and took me out to a Cessna 152. I took off and flew around McAllen for forty minutes. I went over near the B&B, but I realized that the Rio Grande was often masked by trees and the fields on one side of the border couldn't be told from those on the other side. I didn't want to stray into Mexico; that would get me in trouble. I flew back to the airport and drove home. We went to Willie B's, a barbecue place, for lunch. Afterward we picked up some fixings at HEB for a salad and for dinner I poached a piece of salmon which we ate with papaya.

Tuesday 8/29/06

The activity at the feeders has increased. Where three birds had appeared at a feeder earlier, now four or six or eight would be buzzing and twittering, and now three or four birds would feed simultaneously. The slightly larger Buff-bellied Hummingbirds that reside in the Valley seem to have an advantage over the Ruby-throated migrants and bully the smaller birds aside to feed first. But the Ruby-throats are managing to get enough to eat, too, bulking up for their long flight across the Gulf of Mexico to South America.

Wednesday 8/30/06

We went to the wildlife refuge in the morning and arrived before they opened. While we waited, we checked out the ponds outside the grounds and saw a large Texas Indigo Snake swimming toward us. Inside the refuge, the paths down toward the river yielded Green Jays, Cave Swallows, Tropical Kingbirds, a tiny armadillo, a Golden-fronted Woodpecker, an Altamira Oriole, and some Chachalacas. As we walked back up the main path, a couple of Mexican workers building a new observation tower let out some raucous fake tropical bird caws and whoops.

"Hey, guys, what kind of bird is that," they yelled, and laughed.

Reading out by the pool in the afternoon. It seems every time we hang a refilled feeder we find another one empty. This afternoon, carrying out two feeders, I saw there was another that needed filling. Later a male Black-chinned Hummingbird, another migrant, was briefly visible before continuing on his way south. In the evening I found a hummingbird feather on the edge of the pool: a little bit of down at one end and at the other a tiny bit of gold foil or fairy dust.

Thursday 8/31/06

An uneventful morning, but in the middle of the afternoon three Mexicans from Linares in Nuevo Leon showed up at the inner gate of the front wanting water and the use of a phone. They'd hired a coyote in Reynosa for six hundred dollars apiece and he'd left them on the other side of the river. They'd crossed the night before and were supposed to be picked up by a friend, but no one had come. We gave them the water and they called their friend. Then we gave them half a dozen hard-boiled eggs, some tortillas with shredded cheese, and some Bud Lite. J.D. told them to come back if their ride didn't show. Sure enough, in a couple of hours they were back, and this time they asked for a ride to Edinburg, a town north of McAllen, where their friend lived. We took them to a little colonia off Monte Cristo Road and left them in front of a fairly prosperous-looking house. By that time it was already six, so we went back to feed the dogs before going to Alamo to the Mexican restaurant there.

After dark, bats occasionally replaced the hummingbirds at the feeders. One was silently hovering at the nearest one that night as J. D. and I sat out by the pool with a drink. I was worried that what we had done would get back and somehow be a problem for the Taggarts. J. D. reassured me and said he'd told the Mexicans we were only at the B & B for a short time and the owners might well call the Border Patrol if anyone from across the river showed up there.

"Did we do the right thing?" he asked.

"Yes," I said.

Friday 9/1/06

J. D.'s email to a former student, now a lawyer, who, when he learned J.D. and I were spending several weeks on the Texas / Mexico border, said, "I didn't take you for Minutemen":

> Yesterday Mike and I were anti-Minutemen. We were in the pool and the dogs started barking. Three Mexicans were at the gate to our walled hacienda, having slipped over the outside fences. 102 degrees in the shade, and they wanted water. They had come across the border the night before but their "friends" here hadn't picked them up, and they didn't dare to walk along the road just northeast of the river because it is heavily patrolled by the Border Patrol. They were very nice—obviously salt of the earth— and we gave them water and Bud Light (I confess we were trying to get rid of the crap beer that was already in the fridge when we arrived), tacos and hard-boiled eggs, and a phone to make a phone call to a local contact. They waited in the mesquite wood by the road for two hours and nobody came, so they came back and rang the bell, begging for a ride to a nearby city. Cohen and I looked at each other and said yes. So we drove them 30 miles and dropped them off at a friend's house.
>
> I told them that they could thank Our Lady of Guadalupe for this little miracle, because they could have just as easily come to the house of somebody who would have immediately called the BP. They agreed but suggested that it was La Virgen de San Juan instead, because her famous basilica is right around the corner here, and the congregation of that basilica helped their village in Nuevo León build its church recently.
>
> Did we break the law?
>
> Just a vignette of border life.

Saturday 9/2/06

J.D.'s former student wrote back with a chilling little note:

> Section 274 felonies under the federal *Immigration and Nationality Act*, INA 274A (a) (1) (A): "A person...commits a federal felony when she or he...assists an alien s/he should reasonably know is illegally in the U.S....by transporting, sheltering, or assisting him or her to obtain employment, or... knowingly assists illegal aliens due to personal convictions."

Tuesday 9/5/06

We saw a White-tailed Kite in the morning while we were drinking coffee on the patio. We decided to go to Progreso for lunch. In the afternoon, as we were returning, I got out to open the gate. A Mexican came running toward me out of the bosque, smiling, and saying "J.D.? J.D.?" Then another one, a woman, came running out behind him, then another and another and another, until they formed a line across the field and the lawn. I got out and they asked for help and said "J.D?" several times. I said no, but they kept insisting. Then all of them suddenly began running back into the bosque, and I realized that a Border Patrol truck was pulling up behind us. "How many?" asked the patrolman, and I answered "five." He radioed a message and later, after we'd gone into the house, he and another patrolman went into the bosque. I didn't see anyone come back out.

After dark we sat out by the pool again, talking about the day's events.

"I don't think any more will come, do you?" J. D. asked.

"I don't know," I said.

"Have you changed your mind about its being the right thing to do?"

"No," I said.

Thursday 9/7/06

We packed up our things and went to meet Trudy and Jim at the McAllen airport. We went to a Mexican place for lunch, and then they drove J.D. and me back to the airport for our flight out.

Last night I slept badly, and as I was dozing toward morning a musical phrase was playing in my head, the one that Disney used in "The Sorcerer's Apprentice" sequence of *Fantasia.* That's the section where Mickey is the apprentice who's charged with carrying buckets of water to fill the sorcerer's cistern. He picks up the hat the wizard has left behind, puts it on his head, and commands the broom to carry the water buckets instead. But he falls asleep, and when he wakes up the broom has carried so much water the cistern is overflowing. Mickey commands the broom to stop, but nothing happens. He splits it with an axe, but then each part takes on a life of its own and begins to carry more buckets. That was the part that was playing in my dream: endless animated wooden brooms carrying buckets of water that eventually coalesced to become a flood, while the musical phrase ta ta ta ta, ta-ta-duh, ta-ta-DUM, DUM accelerated in tempo and increased in volume.

At the Gym

The first thing that strikes me at my commercial gym is the mirrors, which occupy every wall they can, wherever there is space not taken up by the glass doors that show me what's going on in the handball courts or how fast the stationary cyclists are wheeling in their room or what the Zumba class or the yogistas are getting up to. Here in the weight room, the mirrors stop about knee height to avoid rolling weights smashing them. But in the Zumba/yoga rooms the mirrors go down to within inches from the floor—perhaps because those folks need to see themselves when they're lying on mats, or to see their feet when they're dancing.

Why do they need to see themselves? The argument in the weight room is that a lifter must see that the weights are level and the form correct. An improper lift risks injury. Not everyone buys the argument about reflected form, however. One trainer I talked to said, "Lifters need to be concentrating on the weights. Staring at your bulging muscles in the mirror instead of paying attention is the shortest way to hurt yourself."

A woman friend of mine says some mirrors are just terribly placed: "I myself despise a mirror next to a treadmill. Running is bad enough without having to watch yourself suffering and puffing and sweating along." She is a regular gym goer in good shape. But studies cited by Christina Corcoran in *Psychology Today* (1 August 2003) have shown that women who do not exercise regularly may be deterred from going to the gym by the ubiquitous mirrors.

These observations raise the question, too, about the room with all the bicycles: What is the advantage of watching yourself cycling? Or for that matter Zumba dancing or doing yoga? Is it vanity alone? My friend has noticed "the fellows (often wearing a great deal of cologne, for some reason) who sit down with a weight or two and are just captivated by their own image in the mirror." She points out, too, that mirrors enable a less direct form of people-watching by "the folks who semi-discreetly ogle other folks." Is there a connection between the idea of being fit and the fact of surveillance by self or other? Just asking the question makes it impossible to deny that we're all at the gym to be fit and healthy, which can mean not only feeling good but looking good. Armand Tanny, who with his brother Vic ran one of the first chains of commercial gyms in the country, said "We did a survey…we found the main reason for working out was not for health, but for looking good. That was among both men and women."

*

The omnipresence of commercial gyms is a relatively new phenomenon of American life. We've always had school gyms and, for a couple of centuries, facilities to prepare boxers and other athletes for competition; the New York Athletic Club and its Los Angeles counterpart are examples. But the modern commercial gymnasium and the fitness trend that built it have a more recent history that takes us, like so many American trends and movements, to California for its beginnings.

Marla Matzer Rose argues that it all started in Santa Monica. *In Muscle Beach: Where the Best Bodies in the World Started a Fitness Revolution* (St. Martin's Press, 2001), Rose tells how the 1932 Olympics in Los Angeles sparked local interest in gymnastics. Paul Brewer, a student at Santa Monica High School, was frustrated when the construction of his school's planned gym was delayed on account of the 1933 earthquake, so he and his friends began to exercise on playground equipment on the beach, near the base of Santa Monica Pier, four blocks away from the high school. Local adults helped the kids add a tumbling carpet, parallel bars, and high rings. Over the next few years the area became very popular as a place to practice and show off not only ordinary gymnastics but also group acrobatic routines involving young men and women doing handstands, making human pyramids and towers, and tossing and catching each other. It was a young bunch, attractive and also muscular, since strength training was required for some of these stunts. The people and their activity soon began to be noticed by the beachgoers who flocked to this section on the weekends and christened the place Muscle Beach.

Some of the young people who were regulars began to open their own gyms; others designed and distributed gym equipment that hadn't been available before. Rose argues that participants in Muscle Beach activities, including Jack LaLanne, Vic Tanny and his brother Armand, Joe Gold, George Eiferman, and a dozen others who opened commercial gyms starting in 1936, were responsible for the American fitness trend, which accelerated when servicemen returned from the war in 1945 and has been steadily building since. At intervals over the years, the trend got an additional boost from good publicity. Muscle Beach regulars Buster Crabbe and Steve Reeves had movie careers, while Jane Russell was an occasional visitor to the beach athletic scene. Arnold Schwarzenegger, already a bodybuilder in his native Austria, was an import to a later manifestation of Muscle Beach up the coast in Venice, California, after the original Santa Monica Muscle Beach was closed.

That closure came about at least in part because of a movement from strength and fitness training to an exaggerated emphasis on muscle development. According to Rose's account, there was an intense effort at the weight-lifting aspect of gym activity early in the 1950s, leading to the triumph of the US Olympic weight-lifting team in 1952. This increased interest in weight training was reflected at Muscle Beach. The original athletic group at the beach, whose interest in weight training had been subservient to overall health and acrobatic prowess, gradually dispersed—a lot of them were working hard running their own newly founded gyms—in favor of men who were exclusively weightlifters and body builders. And they were all men, since women's bodybuilding had not yet acquired its later appeal. Not so many people came to Muscle Beach when muscles were all it had to offer. Watching biceps, pecs, and lats grow to what became, especially after the coming of anabolic steroids, exaggerated and even grotesque size turned out to be without the same appeal as watching normally well-muscled men and women having a good time and entertaining the crowds at the same time. Eventually the Santa Monica conservatives, who were more than a little suspicious of the morality of hugely muscled and nearly naked men walking around and flexing for each other, prevailed, and Muscle Beach was shut down.

*

Today, as usual, I spend most of my time at the gym on the treadmill. This particular one, I noticed at my last visit, has "Time Elasped" instead of "Time Elapsed" under the LED readouts on its control board. And before I got on it today, I looked at the other treadmills in this row—they're all Matrix brand machines, and yep, they all say "Elasped." Oh, well, it's physical culture we're here for, though, as Virginia Woolf once wrote, "After all, imagination is largely the child of the flesh." Michel Serres muses in *Variations on the Body* on the splendid physical shape and the "athletic bodies" of Saint Theresa of Avila and Saint Francis of Assissi, who both walked enormous distances in the hilly terrain of their respective countries. "Saintliness follows health" is his speculative conclusion. Certainly, getting my blood flowing seems to clear my thinking, though I doubt it improves my spiritual life. But I like to keep my mind occupied here as well as my body. When I don't have a book to read or to listen to on headphones, my attention and curiosity go out to the people around me.

Gym fashion is as interesting a phenomenon to consider as any. Gym goers often dress as they would to mow the lawn. Shorts are popular, and light T-shirts. An occasional fashionista in a two-toned workout ensemble stands out like a tangerine in a box of rocks. Except for the dedicated body builders in muscle shirts and spandex, there to show out as well as work out, the emphasis is on loose fit and comfort. T-shirts are everywhere, and that means, because some people like to talk with their T-shirts, there are messages.

The gym T-shirt with a message reveals a good deal about the types and their motives for being here. There are belligerent, call-you-out, my-workout-is-better-than-your-workout shirts, which fit with a general trend of insulting texts on clothing tops in or out of gyms. I'm not talking about the narcissistic "God of the Gym" self-promos, but the "Maybe You Should Train as Hard as You Complain" messages.

Most T-shirt injunctions I see are the self-encouraging kind: "No Day Off," "Hustle for the Muscle," and the ones that urge us to bear down: "Better Sore Than Sorry," "Earn Your Shower," and "Sweat Shirt." Some are self-congratulatory, suggesting the shower has already been earned; others, such as "Body Under Construction," hint that there is still work to be done.

The best messages try for humor, from the resigned "Well It's Not Going to Lift Itself" to the hapless "Does Running Late Count as Exercise?" and the perhaps wistful desire to be elsewhere in "Gym and Tonic." Gender matters; few women's shirts talk about quads or lats. "I Don't Sweat, I Sparkle" is popular, with or without glitter. My favorite women's T has a quote from Shakespeare: "Though She Be But Little She Is Fierce." Is there a gender-specific message in "Strong Is The New Sexy?"

*

We're a mixed lot here at the gym. I consider myself among the hard cases: the hurt and the halt and the lame. I discovered after my second back operation that only regular exercise could keep me from back spasm and sciatica, so I am an almost daily communicant here. Others are recovering from joint replacements, fractures, surgeries. The very obese among us have finally had their resolve to lose weight, for so long a mere velleity, energized by grisly warnings from their doctors. I come often enough to watch progress in my fellow gym goers, including real weight loss and the return of muscle tone. Most, alas, I don't see after a few visits; they have either lost heart or gone to a better gym.

The fitness bunch are largely young people who use the aerobic machines with occasional short visits to the weight room. Some of these are athletes, here because their regular training places are unavailable for some reason: it may be a holiday, or *they're* on a holiday away from home. The others in this group are not athletes but just like to stay fit. My estimate is that young women predominate in the fitness bunch. But for men and women alike, the gym can be part of their discipline to control their weight as well. And they may be here just because of the general good feeling and energy regular exercise gives.

The "muscle batch" is what I'm calling the denizens of the weight room whose efforts look to me to be exclusively aimed at building muscle. I consider them the oddest specimens here, though you might say this is a house they and their kind built. They come out of the weight room and wander the rest of the gym sometimes to cool off or just to display, but I rarely see them on the treadmills, stair-steppers, elliptical trainers, or stationary bicycles that make up the cardio machine section.

There are young men here who look like the Greek paragon visible in statues of the *kouros*, an idealized figure of a youth who is moderately muscled, wide at the shoulders, narrow at the hips. But for many in the weight room, it seems that ideal is not enough, and they go past perfection to a stage where biceps, chest, and shoulders look not so much developed as inflated.

It's my impression that most of the muscle-batch guys are shorter than I am. At five feet nine, I am a half inch below the current American male average height, according to the CDC's 2010 Anthropometric Reference Data. Interestingly, Marla Matzer Rose says a lot of the men in the original Muscle Beach crowd were small.

I sometimes see men here who apparently work on upper-body strength to the exclusion of everything else, so a fellow with large biceps, pectoral and abdominal muscles seems to be walking around on spindly legs. But then a second take tells me the legs are perfectly normal but just look attenuated by comparison with the hyperdeveloped upper body. Differential bodybuilding in men shows up all around me in barrel-chested guys who've worked hard on biceps and other arm muscles but who have prominent bellies.

The women who spend a lot of time in the weight room develop upper-body muscle, but never approaching the bulging biceps of the men. Some have prominent gluteal muscles and a tendency toward frog thighs. I can only guess that within this body culture the look is perceived as sexy. At any rate, it seems to be *sought*. I suspect that women who visit the gym on a casual basis regard the machines that work hip and thigh muscles as slimming. The muscle culture women know better and are cultivating muscular thighs and glutes. Personally, I find the muscled butt unsexy, looking steatopygous rather than toned, a muscle-bustle.

The subject of who's attractive in the gym leads me to a favorite people-watching activity here: looking at the couples. Lots of couples come to the gym. "My favorite pair," says my woman friend, "is an elderly couple that shows up together and maneuvers from one machine to the next, very slowly, she coaching him and he listening very carefully to her." The fitness couples may come in together, but they usually split up right away, each with a program in mind. I will sometimes see him join her when she's almost finished with her run on the treadmill, or vice-versa.

The muscle-batch couples occasionally have separate routines also, but the pairs that interest me are the ones who work out together, he showing her how it's done with the big numbers on the resistance setting, then scaling them back for her workout on the same machine, and finally giving her little tips about form as she does the same routine. The couple I'm watching at the moment is one muscled guy accompanied by an equally strong-looking and slightly taller woman. Today

I've also seen a couple at the resistance machines consisting of a large man and a woman half his size.

When I consider these romances seemingly growing out of a mutual love of physical culture, I can't help wondering whether the romantic passion and the passion for body toning are equal on both sides. Could one of the lovers have a less avid love for the clean and jerk than the bill and coo? Does she—or possibly he—go to the gym so often just because the other wants to?

There is another book with the title *Muscle Beach*, but this one is a novel, written by Ira Wallach in 1959. Wallach tells the story of a muscle-building couple, Jocie and Harry. The narrator of the novel is a New Yorker transplanted to California, named Carlo. Carlo sees Jocie on the beach and becomes infatuated with her perfect body. By means of deception and guile, Carlo succeeds in detaching Jocie from Harry, and for a while, he imagines that he's got his dream girl. But Jocie and Harry are thinking about each other when they're not thinking about their own bodies, and when Jocie leaves to rejoin Harry, Carlo is a little sad, but he grasps the inevitable mutual magnetism of the pair.

*

"Let nothing divert you from your duty to your body," advises Walt Whitman, who wrote a column on "Manly Health and Training" for *The New York Atlas* in 1858. Though nothing like the modern commercial gym was available to him—and he preferred the open air anyway—Whitman endorsed using weights, boxing, sparring or punching a heavy bag, walking, swimming, rowing, jumping jacks, climbing—even dancing—as exercise. It's fair to say that Whitman's enthusiasm for vigorous exercise leads him to exaggerate its virtues. He claims that "natural moral goodness is developed in proportion with a sound physical development." Exercise often goes to people's heads, as when Michael Serres says it is allied to saintliness. Whitman, with characteristic self-admiration, thinks it also makes him handsome—"yes, handsome—for it is not for nothing that all through the human race there is the universal desire that the body should not only be well, but look well." And this brings me back to the mirrors.

I reject the interior decorators' banal explanation that the mirrors are there to make the rooms look larger; the truly enormous gyms are the ones with the most mirrors. No, the mirrors are there so we can look at ourselves. The gym experience is all about self-regard. We're all at the gym because we have looked at ourselves: literally in a mirror, or in the mind's reflecting on our state of muscle tone, energy, endurance. We have looked at ourselves and decided we want to find or preserve something in us: decrease a belly or augment a bicep; make a joint more mobile or a back stronger. Even for the least vain among us, the mirrors serve a purpose. My woman friend, who has just finished her run on the treadmill, picks up her bag and gives a little smile to her reflection in the mirror by the door as she leaves.

Tucson Time

To illustrate the way the mind can hold past and present together at once, Freud begins *Civilization and Its Discontents* (1930) with a striking image. Imagine looking at the city of Rome, he invites us, and being able to see *all* the buildings that have ever been there, at once, past and present: the palaces of the Caesars, the Temple of Jupiter Capitolinus as well as the building that replaced it, Nero's Golden House and the Coliseum occupying the same space at the same time, Etruscan structures in the same view as the edifices that were built on their ruined foundations, and so on.

At times I see Tucson this way, as a palimpsest where the layers are transparent and what lies beneath is visible even while I read the writing on the surface. Jacome's department store and Steinfeld's facing each other across Pennington on Stone and, across Stone, the Pioneer Hotel before the fire are visible to me in my mind's eye as I look at the buildings there now, or their absence in Jacomé Park. Jacome's closed in 1980, and Steinfeld's had been demolished six years earlier. That was four years after the fire in the Pioneer that killed Harold and Margaret Steinfeld in their penthouse apartment. When the hotel was redone as an office building, its façade completely changed, that little section of downtown Tucson had been transformed as if by Neronic fire and rebuilding.

Less dramatic change transforms much more mundane edifices as well. When I pass the Moose Lodge on Ruthrauff, I think of its last incarnation as Country West, where my wife Katharine and I stopped the night Johnny Cash died to hear that day's band play their homage to his music. Before that, Country West had been The Branding Iron, if memory serves. Memory, and sometimes the archives of *The Arizona Star*, can be all I have in these reconstructions.

In the last year one of the old watering holes closed: the Rusty Nail, on Wetmore and Flowing Wells, shut its doors for good after 44 years of dispensing reasonably-priced booze to its patrons. The last tap on the rusty nail started me thinking of other, more familiar dives that are no more. The first of these to go was the Green Dolphin on Park. Aside from the pool table that always had quarters sitting on the rail indicating players in line to use it next, the major attraction of the Green Dolphin was its closeness to the University of Arizona. In those days—the place was active from the 1960s to the 80s—there was no string of bars on 3rd (now called University) Street at the college gates. I suppose the Green Dolphin attracted a fairly eclectic group of students, but I always remember the place in the mid-sixties as being full of Anthropology and English graduate students. As the closing hour approached—it was one a.m. in those days—the serious drinkers would line up at the bar for depth charges—shot glasses of whiskey dropped into glasses of beer—or beer and tequila shots. From several parts of the room would come a badly harmonized version of "the Athabascan bastards caused the Great Pueblo's fall."

By the late 80s, the Green Dolphin's trade was being squeezed by bars closer to the dorms, and in the early 90s I read in the *Star* that the owner had committed suicide in the building after going bankrupt.

My memory says—and the *Star* is no help here—that four or six pool tables were an attraction at the Grant Road Tavern, which was also cleaner, better lighted (some like those sorts of things) and with a slightly tonier clientele, although one day my friend Bob Ackerman and I heard the two guys at an adjoining pool table discussing their recent release from jail and their next move. "We could steal a car," said one of them.

The Grant Road Tavern burned in 1987. Shaffer Mabarak, who owned half a dozen Tucson bars at one time or another, chose not to rebuild. I think it's interesting that when the Star published his obituary in 1999, Mabarak's owning of the Grant Road Tavern showed up in the first couple of sentences.

Some bars just stay there while the area around them morphs into something else. The oldest bar in Tucson still operating in the same location is The Buffet, which began life as The Lantern Buffet when it was built in 1934 to serve railroad workers from the depot nearby. The depot is long gone, and the area is now a sedate lower-middle-class neighborhood, while The Buffet has settled into a neighborhood bar that just happens to have its walls completely covered with graffiti layered like a palimpsest.

*

In Tucson, when you see a big stand of the tall, thin palms called Washingtonians, you're probably close to one of the city's old trailer parks. The slenderest and tallest of the palms are a naturally occurring species in the Sonoran Desert, *Washingtonia robusta*, which can reach eighty or ninety feet high. A slightly thicker and shorter variety, the California fan palm, *Washingtonia filifera*, can be found all over Tucson as well, but has less of the slim elegance of *robusta*, which is sometimes called the Mexican fan palm.

The settled communities that these old trailer parks have become defies the association of transience and impermanence trailers have. There are 430 trailer parks in the county, representing ten percent of the living spaces. Many of them exist because about a quarter of Arizona families spend more than half their income on housing, and trailers are an answer to that huge economic bite. But the culture of the long-established trailer parks is that of an older, more well-off, and economically more stable crowd. They live in trailer parks, yes, but ones that have become settled communities, rivaling neighborhoods of pre-WWII houses, and adorned with some of the oldest and most magnificent tall palms to be found in the city. Some of the people in these parks may still be winter residents only, but a lot of them clearly decided a long time ago that this was the place to be year-round.

Not as visible as the palms from a distance but usually bordering these parks, equally aged and impressive, are the Burbank prickly pears that massively hedge and enclose them.

At the beginning of the twentieth century Luther Burbank hybridized two Mexican varieties of prickly pear to produce these cacti. Burbank was looking for a cactus that could feed cattle, and found it. But in this part of Arizona people saw these heavy, substantial, thornless cacti as good substitutes for hedges and fences. Occasionally a property owner would back up a line of Burbanks with a simple post-and-rail fence. But with or without the fence, the arrangement required little maintenance and the plants needed no water beyond the sparse desert rainfall.

Tall palm and giant prickly-pear trailer parks are not everywhere in Tucson, but there are enough to be familiar landmarks in the cityscape. Another kind of flora, less conspicuous from a distance but equally old, marks a separate group of trailer parks.

I suppose the palm and cactus plantings were appealing to those ready to embrace the move to the southwest from wherever they came. But a park with more greenery might have appealed to people not ready for a clean break with the grass and shrubs of the states they left behind. And there are parks in Tucson where the plants, though as old as the cactus and palms in other parks, offered more shade and verdant prospects. Typical of the latter is a trailer park on Limberlost Drive called Vista del Norte—and it does indeed have a splendid view of the Santa Catalina Mountains to the north. This park is bordered with the tallest oleanders I've ever seen. I think they may be twenty feet tall, and they challenge the overhead phone and electrical wires in places. Twenty feet is the maximum height for oleanders, according to the scientific literature.

These are white-flowering oleanders. Red and pink ones are popular elsewhere in town, but almost all the old ones I see are white. *Nerium oleander* is so widely cultivated that no one knows in what part of the world it originated, but it was probably somewhere in south Asia. Like the palm and cacti, oleander is also drought-resistant, though it needs some watering beyond the local rainfall, and it is not easily swept away in gully-washers when the rains do come. When it grows to these sizes it is virtually opaque to prying eyes and thus functions well as a boundary hedge.

Possibly the only disadvantage of the plant is that all of its part are toxic to people and some animals. A fanciful etymology has its name deriving from the Greek ολλυω ανδρα, "I kill man."

Vista del Norte also has some very large eucalyptus trees. This is the Australian *coolibah*, the tree under which the swagman camped in "Waltzing Matilda." *Eucalyptus microtheca* has been a very popular import in southern Arizona because it grows fast and resists heat. The tree is dense enough to be useful for shade and as a windbreak, like the oleander.

Surrounded by palm and cactus or by oleander and eucalyptus, the folks in these trailer parks have been living there long enough to qualify as real desert rats—a term of affection around here. Children and grandchildren have been born and have grown up while these plantings around them also matured. Now the palms, oleander and eucalyptus are tall enough to be landmarks and as elegant in their way as the landscaping in much richer neighborhoods.

*

From my vantage point to their west, the Santa Catalina Mountains turn pink at sundown. A friend says, "Mountains are pink; time for a drink." Some effect of horizontal light, no doubt. The effect is quite dramatic, since these are not red sandstone, but granite formations. What in Europe would be called *die blaue Stunde* because of the intensifying blue of the sky at dusk is here an effect at the other end of the spectrum. But then this is the desert, and we should expect hot colors.

At this point in late July the only blossoms in evidence are the yellows, oranges, and reds of the barrel cactus. These same colors blazed in stands of cholla—called cholla gardens—during the spring. Sometimes the colors came all in one package. We have a variety of cholla, *Cylindropuntia versicolor*, the staghorn cholla, whose red, orange, yellow, yellow-green, pink, and bronze blossoms can occasionally appear on the same plant. All my life I have seen the yellow blossoms of Palo Verde trees, of creosote bushes, and of prickly pear cactus, the red-to-yellow spectrum of cholla blossoms, the orange-red torches of ocotillo, and it never occurred to me how few things bloom in the desert with colors from the other end of the spectrum. True, there are tiny blue wildflowers like Chicory or Lupine, and there is of course the Purple Sage. But the real desert plants—the ones who take the heat all the year round—don't have cool colors.

The Saguaro blooms are white, but they are soon followed by the startling red of the fruits. I say startling because one can look up at a White-winged Dove feasting on the blood-red fruit and be shocked into suspecting that the peaceful Columbid has turned predator and is ripping its prey apart up there on the spiny top of the cactus.

References

Venues for those essays that have been previously published are acknowledged below. The author wishes to thank the editors of the journals where they appeared for permission to reprint them and for their generous help in revision for first publication. Sources are listed below for quotations, citations, and illustrations in the order they appear in the text. The author asserts fair use privilege with acknowledgments for short quotations.

Preface

John Keats, "On First Looking into Chapman's Homer."
Conversations with Jorge Luis Borges, recorded by Richard Burgin (Holt, Rinehart and Winston, 1969).

Don't Read the Whole Thing

John Rawls, *A Theory of Justice* (Harvard University Press, 1971).
Sir Francis Bacon, "Of Studies," *Essays* (1625).
William L. Shirer, *The Rise and Fall of the Third Reich: A History of Nazi Germany* (Simon and Schuster, 1960).

The Cross and the Windmills [was published in *Evening Street Review* 25 (Autumn 2020)]

Talking to Myself [published in *North Dakota Quarterly*, 87:1/2 (Spring/Summer 2020), 72-77]

Bob Dylan, "You're Gonna Make Me Lonesome When You Go," Blood on the Tracks (Columbia, 1975).
Charles Fernyhough, The Voices Within: The History and Science of How We Talk to Ourselves (The Wellcome Collection/Profile, 2016).
The Son of Sam confessions are related in Kim Rossmo, *Geographic Profiling* (CRC, 1999).

On dialogue with the self, see William James, *The Principles of Psychology* (1890) and Mikhail Bakhtin, *The Dialogic Imagination: Four Essays* (Texas, 1982). On dialogical self theory, see, for example J. J. M Hermans and H. J. G. Kempen, *The Dialogical Self: Meaning as Movement* (Academic Press, 1993).

Carol Marie Kronk, "Private Speech in Adolescents," *Adolescence*, vol. 29-116 (1994) 781-804.

Daniel Swingley and Gary Lupyan, "Self-directed speech affects visual search performance," in the 2011 *The Quarterly Journal of Experimental Psychology*, vol. 65-6, (2012) 1068-1085.

Ethan Kross et al., "Self-Talk as a Regulatory Mechanism: How You Do It Matters," *Journal of Personality and Social Psychology*, vol. 106-2 (2014) 304-324.

Antonis Hatzigeorgiadis, Nikos Zourbanos, Evangelos Galanis, and Yiannis Theodorakis, "Self-Talk and Sports Performance: a Meta-Analysis," *Perspectives on Psychological Science* 6-4 (2011) 348-356.

Émile Coué, *Self Mastery Through Conscious Autosuggestion* (Malkan Publishing, 1922).

George Pólya, *How To Solve It: A New Aspect of Mathematical Method* (Princeton, 1945).

Why Didn't Our Big Brains Save Us? [complete references in this essay appear parenthetically in the text]

Just a Note in Haste [appeared in *Burningword 92* (October 2019)]

Virginia Woolf's review of Walpole's letters is in *The Essays of Virginia Woolf*, six volumes (Hogarth Press, 1986-2011).

In Tearing Haste: Letters between Deborah Devonshire and Patrick Leigh Fermor (John Murray, 2008).

"The Galaxy Song," Eric Idle and John Du Prez, as sung by Eric Idle in Monty Python's *The Meaning of Life* (1983) and Clint Black on *D'lectrified* (1999).

Almost Enough Caviar [published in *Ascent* (January 9, 2014) and nominated for a Pushcart Prize]

M. F. K. Fisher, *With Bold Knife and Fork* (G. P. Putnam's Sons, 1969).

A. J. Liebling, *The Sweet Science: A Ringside View of Boxing* (Grove Press, 1949).

Jonathan Lehrer, *Proust Was a Neuroscientist* (Houghton Mifflin Harcourt, 2007).

Adam Gopnik, *Paris to the Moon* (Random House, 2000).

Julia Child, Louisette Bertholle, and Simone Beck, *Mastering the Art of French Cooking* (Knopf, 1961).

Inés and Simone Ortega, *1080 Recipes* (1972, English edition Phaidon, 2007).

Myra Waldo, *Cook As the Romans Do* (Collier Books, 1961).

Jean Anthelme Brillat-Savarin, *The Physiology of Taste: Or, Meditations on Transcendental Gastronomy*, translated by M. F. K. Fisher (Heritage Press, 1949).

Getting Past the ABCs [appeared in a slightly different version in *AirFacts* (June 12, 2014)]

FAR/AIM: *Federal Aviation Regulations/Aeronautical Information Manual* (Aviation Supplies & Academics, Inc., published every year).

Agonists [was published in a slightly different form in *The Missouri Review*, 31:2 (Summer 2008)]

Nancy Mairs, "On Being a Cripple," *Plaintext* (Arizona, 1986).

—, *Voice Lessons: On Becoming a (Woman) Writer* (Beacon Press, 1994).

Joyce Carol Oates, "Against Nature," *The Ontario Review* (1986). Reprinted in Donald Hall, ed., *The Contemporary Essay*, 2nd edition (St. Martin's, 1989).

Joan Didion, *The Year of Magical Thinking* (Knopf, 2005).

—, "In Bed." *The White Album* (Noonday, 1990).

Michel de Montaigne, "Of the Affection of Fathers for Their Children," in *The Complete Works of Montaigne: Essays, Travel Journals, Letters*. Translated and introduced by Donald M. Frame (Stanford University Press, 1958).

Charles Lamb, *Confessions of a Drunkard* (1813).

Barry Cornwall, *Charles Lamb: A Memoir* (1866).

Thomas De Quincey, *Confessions of an English Opium-Eater* (1821).

Caroline Knapp. *Drinking: A Love Story* (Dial Press, 1996).

Caroline Knapp, *Appetites: Why Women Want* (Counterpoint, 2003).

—, *The Merry Recluse: A Life in Essays*, edited by Sandra Shea (Counterpoint, 2004).

Marjorie Williams, *The Woman at the Washington Zoo: Writings on Politics, Family, and Fate*, edited by Timothy Noah (Public Affairs, 2005).

Andre Dubus, *Broken Vessels* (Godine, 1991).

—, *Meditations from a Movable Chair: Essays* (Knopf, 1998).

James Frey, *A Million Little Pieces* (Doubleday, 2003).

C.S. Lewis, *A Grief Observed* (Faber & Faber, 1961).

Certificates

Sherwin B. Nuland, *How We Die: Reflections on Life's Final Chapter* (Knopf, 1994).

Herman Melville, *The Confidence-Man: His Masquerade* (Dix, Edwards, 1857).

O. Henry [William Sydney Porter], *The Gentle Grafter* (Doubleday, 1908).

Sorry, But I Like Air Travel

George Carlin on the vocabulary of airlines and flying: https://www.youtube.com/watch?v=vdPy5Ikn7dw

Virginia Woolf, in a review of *Château and Country Life in France*, by Mary King Waddington, in the *Times Literary Supplement* (29 October 1908).

The God Damners [published in *SKEPTIC* magazine, 23:4 (2018)]

Samuel Harris, *The End of Faith: Religion, Terror, and the Future of Reason* (Norton, 2004).

—, *Letter to a Christian Nation* (Knopf, 2006).

Richard Dawkins, *The God Delusion* (Bantam, 2006).

Daniel C. Dennett, *Breaking the Spell: Religion as a Natural Phenomenon* (Viking/Penguin, 2006).

—, *Darwin's Dangerous Idea* (Simon & Schuster, 1995).

Christopher Hitchens, *God Is Not Great: How Religion Poisons Everything* (Twelve Books, 2007).

"The fool hath said in his heart, There is no God," Psalms 13:1 and 53:1, *King James Version of the Bible.*

Thomas Paine, *The Age of Reason* (1794).

Charles Darwin, *The Origin of Species* (1859).

Bertrand Russell, "Why I Am Not a Christian" (1927) in *Why I Am Not a Christian: and Other Essays on Religion and Related Subjects* (Routledge, 1943).

H. L. Mencken, *Treatise on the Gods* (Knopf, 1930).

Sigmund Freud, *The Future of an Illusion* (1927; Liveright 1949).

—, *Civilization and Its Discontents* (1930; Hogarth Press, 1949).

—, *Totem and Taboo* (1913; Routledge, 1919).

Stephen Jay Gould discusses "non-overlapping magisteria" in *Rocks of Ages: Science and Religion in the Fullness of Life* (Ballantine Books, 1999).

David Hume, "On Miracles," section X of *An Enquiry concerning Human Understanding* (1748).

Blaise Pascal's discussion of his wager occurs in section 233 of the *Pensées* (1670).

Albert Einstein writes in a letter to Guy Raner (September 28, 1949) that he thinks the notion of a personal God is childlike, but that he is not an atheist.

Orwell's remark about totalitarianism and theocracy was first published in an essay, "The Prevention of Literature," in *Polemic* (No. 2, 1946) and reprinted in his later essay collections.

The London Independent reported the Gog-Magog comment of George W. Bush, and Chirac later confirmed it in an interview with Jean-Claude Maurice, Si Vous le Répétez, Je Démentirai (Plon, 2009).

Trains, Ships, and Trucks

The Canyon, the Collision, and the Kid Who Liked to Fly [appeared in *The Chattahoochee Review* 40.2, (Fall 2020)]

Walker Percy, "The Loss of the Creature," *Forum 2* (Fall, 1958).

Joseph Heller, *Catch-22* (Simon & Schuster, 1961).

Mariana Gosnell, *Zero Three Bravo: Solo Across America in a Small Plane* (Simon & Schuster, 1993).

The Materialist in Her Bathtub [appeared in *The Humanist* (May/June 2014)]

Mary McCarthy, "America the Beautiful," *On the Contrary* (Farrar, Straus and Cudahy, 1951).

Joan Didion, *Slouching Towards Bethlehem* (Farrar, Straus and Giroux, 1968).

Oscar Wilde, *The Importance of Being Earnest* (1895).

E. M. Forster, "My Wood," *Abinger Harvest* (Edward Arnold, 1936).

Henry David Thoreau, *Walden; Or, Life in the Woods* (1854).

George Carlin, "Stuff": https://www.youtube.com/watch?v=MvgN5gCuLac&list=RDMvgN5gCuLac.

Ernest Hemingway, "Big Two-Hearted River," *Our Time* (Boni & Liveright, 1925).

James A. Roberts, *Shiny Objects: Why We Spend Money We Don't Have in Search of Happiness We Can't Buy* (HarperOne, 2011).

Alexis de Tocqueville, *Democracy in America* (1835).

The Maltese Falcon and *The Great American Novel* [published in *Able Muse 26* (Winter 2018)]

Dashiell Hammett, *The Maltese Falcon* (Knopf, 1930).

Travels with Pat [published in a shorter form in *Cumberland River Review*, 8.2 (April 2019)]

The Epic of Gilgamesh, translated by N. K. Sandars (Penguin Classics, 1972).

Virginia Woolf, "Montaigne," in *The Common Reader* (Hogarth Press, 1925).

Donald Frame's "Introduction" and Montaigne's essay "On Friendship," in *The Complete Works of Montaigne: Essays, Travel Journals, Letters.* Translated and introduced by Donald M. Frame (Stanford University Press, 1958).

Adam Gopnik, "Montaigne on Trial," *The New Yorker* (16 January 2017).

Plato's Handbook

Walt Disney's *Uncle Scrooge #5*, *#12*, and *#18*, Cal Barks, Dell

Publishing (1955).

Boy Scout Handbook, 12th edition, (Boy Scouts of America, 2009).

Paul Fussell, "The Boy Scout Handbook," in *The Boy Scout Handbook and Other Observations* (Oxford University Press, 1982).

"Scout protecting child from mad dog," Boy Scouts of America: *The Official Handbook for Boys* (1911).

Drawing of duck profiles, Ernest Thompson Seton, *Two Little Savages* (1903).

Roger Tory Peterson, *A Field Guide to the Birds* (Houghton Mifflin, 1934).

Chandler S. Robbins, Bertel Braun, and Herbert S. Zim, *Birds of North America: A Guide to Field Identification*, Illustrated by Arthur Singer (Golden Press, 1966).

Multiple Authors, *Field Guide to the Birds of North America* (National Geographic, 1983).

David Allen Sibley, *The Sibley Guide to Birds: National Audubon Society* (Knopf, 2000).

Title page, Anna Botsford Comstock, *Handbook of Nature Study* (Cornell University Press, 1918).

Roseann Beggy Hanson and Jonathan Hanson, *Southern Arizona Nature Almanac* (University of Arizona Press, 2003).

Learning Ancient Greek at the Downtown Y [published in *Concho River Review*, 34:1 (Spring/Summer 2020)]

Homer, *Odyssey*, translated by E. V. Rieu (Penguin Classic, 1946).

—, *The Odyssey of Homer*, translated by Richmond Lattimore (Harper & Row, 1967).

—, The Odyssey, translated by Robert Fagles (Viking, 1996).

Peter Jones, *Learn Ancient Greek: A Lively Introduction to Learning the Language* (Duckworth, 1998).

Hans-Friedrich Mueller, *Greek 101: Learning an Ancient Language* (The Teaching Company, 2016).

W. S. Merwin, "Learning a Dead Language," *The Rain in the Trees* (Knopf, 1988).

National Institute for Aging in the National Institutes of Health: https://www.nia.nih.gov/health/cognitive-health.

Playing Golf *versus* Reading About It

William Matthews," Foul Shots: A Clinic," in *Rising and Falling* (Little Brown, 1978).

Tommy Armour, *How to Play Your Best Golf All the Time* (Simon & Schuster, 1953).

Robert Tyre Jones, *Bobby Jones on Golf* (Doubleday, 1966).

Arnold Palmer, *My Game and Yours* (Simon and Schuster, 1965).

Ben Hogan, with Herbert Warren Wind, *Five Lessons: The Modern Fundamentals of Golf* (Simon and Schuster, 1957).

Jack Nicklaus, with Ken Bowden, *Golf My Way* (Simon and Schuster, 1974).

Tiger Woods, with the editors of Golf Digest, *How I Play Golf* (Grand Central Publishing, 2001).

Corey Pavin, with Guy Yocom, *Corey Pavin's Shotmaking* (Simon and Schuster, 1996).

Nick Faldo, with Richard Simmons, *A Swing for Life* (Penguin, 1995).

Advice on Writing Your Suicide Note [appeared in *Just Off Message: A 20th Year Anthology,* edited by David P. Reiter (Interactive Press, 2017)]

George Sanders, suicide note quoted at http://classicmoviechat.com/george-sanders-bored-to-death/

Thomas Hardy, *Jude the Obscure* (1895).

Virginia Woolf, suicide note quoted with photo of the note at https://en.wikisource.org/wiki/Virginia_Woolf_suicide_note

Benjamin Alsup, "Saint David Foster Wallace and *The Pale King*," *Esquire* (March 15, 2011).

David Foster Wallace, "Graduate Address to the Kenyon College Class of 2005," https://fs.blog/2012/04/david-foster-wallace-this-is-water/.

Johnny Mandel and Mike Altman, "Suicide Is Painless," (1970) Columbia/CBS.

Dorothy Parker, "Resumé," *Enough Rope* (Horace Liveright, 1926).

A Chance Conversation [published in *Cumberland River Review* 6:4 (October 2017)]

Alexandre Dumas, *The Three Musketeers* (1844).

Virginia Woolf, *Jacob's Room* (Hogarth Press, 1922).

—, *To the Lighthouse* (Hogarth Press, 1927).

Stephen Jay Gould, *Wonderful Life: The Burgess Shale and the Nature of History* (Norton, 1989).

Wallace Stevens, "The Idea of Order at Key West," *Ideas of Order* (Knopf, 1935).

Joseph Conrad, *Chance* (1913).

Sir Thomas Browne, *Religio Medici* (1643).

E. M. Forster, *Aspects of the Novel* (Edward Arnold, 1927).

Dashiell Hammett, *The Maltese Falcon* (Knopf, 1930).

Francis Bacon, "Of Fortune," *Essays* (1625).

Thomas Hardy, "Hap," Wessex Poems and Other Verses (1898).

Wallace Stevens, "Anecdote of the Jar," *Collected Poems* (Knopf, 1923, 1951, 1954).

Paris from the Terrace

A. J. Liebling, *Between Meals* (Simon & Schuster, 1962).

Ernest Hemingway, *A Moveable Feast* (Scribners, 1964).

Raymond Queneau, *Zazie in the Metro*, translated by Barbara Wright (Bodley Head, 1959).

Janet Flanner, *Paris Was Yesterday 1925-1939* (Viking, 1972).

Adam Gopnik, *Paris to the Moon* (Random House, 2000).

The Road to Beatrice

Oliver Goldsmith, "The Deserted Village: A Poem," (W. Griffin, 1770)

South Texas Diary, 2006

Bruce Springsteen, "Across the Border." Downtown Music Publishing/BMG (1995).

The Immigration and Nationality Act of 1965: https://www.uscis.gov/legal-resources/immigration-and-nationality-act

Walt Disney Productions, *Fantasia* (1940).

At the Gym [published in *The Missouri Review* online (August 2019)]

Christina Corcoran, "Mirror, Mirror in the Gym," *Psychology Today* (1 August 2003). Corcoran cites a study by Kathleen A. Martin Ginis, an associate professor of kinesiology at McMaster University in Ontario, Canada, published in *Health Psychology*.

Marla Matzer Rose, *Muscle Beach: Where the Best Bodies in the World Started a Fitness Revolution* (St. Martin's Press, 2001).

Michel Serres, *Variations on the Body*, translated by Randolph Burks (University of Minnesota Press, 2011).

Ira Wallach, *Muscle Beach* (Little, Brown, 1959).

The Walt Whitman quotes from his 1858 *The New York Atlas* columns may be found in Walt Whitman's *Guide to Manly Health and Training* (Ten Speed Press, 2017).

Tucson Time

Sigmund Freud, *Civilization and Its Discontents* (1930; Hogarth Press, 1949).

"The Great Athabascan Migration," sung to the tune of "The Wabash Cannonball," was supposedly composed in the Anthropology Department at the University of Arizona by Don Scheans to celebrate the PhD dissertation of Ned Swanson, according to Roger Tibbetts Grange, Jr.'s book, *A Funny Thing Happened on the Way to the Dig: An Archaeologist's Autobiography* (BookBaby, 2017).